LIVE RIGHT and FIND HAPPINESS

(Although Beer Is Much Faster)

ALSO BY DAVE BARRY

FICTION

Insane City

Lunatics (with Alan Zweibel)

The Bridge to Never Land (with Ridley Pearson)

Peter and the Sword of Mercy (with Ridley Pearson)

Science Fair (with Ridley Pearson)

Peter and the Secret of Rundoon (with Ridley Pearson)

Cave of the Dark Wind (with Ridley Pearson)

The Shepherd, the Angel, and Walter the Christmas Miracle Dog

Escape from the Carnivale (with Ridley Pearson)

Peter and the Shadow Thieves (with Ridley Pearson)

Peter and the Starcatchers (with Ridley Pearson)

Tricky Business

Big Trouble

NONFICTION

LIVE RIGHT and FIND HAPPINESS

(Although Beer Is Much Faster)

✴ ✴ ✴

Life Lessons and Other Ravings
from Dave Barry

Dave Barry

G. P. PUTNAM'S SONS | *New York*

G. P. PUTNAM'S SONS
Publishers Since 1838
Published by the Penguin Group
Penguin Group (USA) LLC
375 Hudson Street
New York, New York 10014

USA • Canada • UK • Ireland • Australia
New Zealand • India • South Africa • China

penguin.com
A Penguin Random House Company

ISBN 978-0-399-16595-5

Printed in the United States of America
1   3   5   7   9   10   8   6   4   2

BOOK DESIGN BY NICOLE LAROCHE

CONTENTS

LIVE RIGHT and FIND HAPPINESS

INTRODUCTION

What makes us happy?

It's definitely not money. To quote the old saying that old people are always saying: "Money can't buy happiness."

How very true that is.

Oh, you might *think* money would make you happy. But would it really? Let's say you inherited a billion dollars. You could have a private jet, live in a mansion with a swimming pool, drive a Maserati. You could drive your Maserati into your swimming pool if you felt like it. That's how rich you'd be.

But would all that money really make you happy? Would your family and friends really love you any more?

OK, they probably would, especially if you let them ride

in your jet. And if they *didn't* love you more, you could afford to have them professionally whacked and get a whole new set of family and friends. People would *audition* to be your friend. I would be one of these people.

So apparently the old saying is wrong: Money *can* buy you happiness. The problem is, you need a really large quantity of it. You have to be one of those twenty-three-year-old Internet billionaires that everybody would like to punch in the mouth.

So most of us have to seek happiness in other ways. Tragically, some people turn to drugs or alcohol. This is a big mistake. I realize that the title of this book seems to suggest that you can achieve happiness by drinking beer, but that is of course a joke. Beer is not the answer. Sure, when your problems are getting you down, drinking beer might *temporarily* improve your mood. But what happens when the beer wears off? You're right back where you started, still stuck with all the same problems. Sooner or later, you're going to have to face the harsh truth: *You need more beer.*

No! Strike that. The harsh truth is that happiness is an elusive thing. I speak from personal experience here. I should be a happy man. I have all the elements of a good life: a loving family, a nice home, a dog that doesn't pee indoors without a good reason. I have a full head of hair and several original teeth. I have no major health issues that I am aware of, thanks to a rigorous healthcare regimen of never getting within 200 yards of a known healthcare provider. I have a small group of really close male friends with whom I am not in touch because we are males, but I know I can count on them if I ever really need them, assuming they are still alive.

And if all of that isn't enough, I've had a long and rewarding career that consists of being paid to write pretty much any random idiot thing I want. You can put suspenders on a salamander, but it still won't make waffles. See what I mean? That sentence makes absolutely no sense, but *I got paid to write it*. It's printed right here in a published book! Unless you're a high-ranking federal official, there is no way you can do anything this useless and still have a job.

So I have been blessed with many blessings. I should be happy. And I am, sort of. But I can't escape the nagging feeling that I'm not *really* happy, at least not the way I was when I was young and carefree and basically an idiot.

I especially have this feeling when it's my turn to drive the soccer practice car pool for my daughter, Sophie, and some of her teammates. This involves spending up to an hour in a confined space with a group of fourteen- and fifteen-year-old girls, all high school freshmen, listening to them discuss the concerns that girls of that age have, such as racism, bullying and global climate change.

I am of course kidding. Here are the top ten concerns of my daughter and her friends, based on their car pool conversations:

1. Boys.
2. The hideous totally unwarranted cruelty of high school teachers.
3. What this one boy did in this one class OMG.
4. Some video on some Internet thing that is HILARIOUS.
5. Hair.

6–10. Boys.

All of the girls discuss all of these topics simultaneously at high volume while at the same time (they are excellent multi-taskers) thumbing away on their phones and listening to the radio, which is cranked way up so they can hear it over the noise they're making.

So they're very loud. They're spooking cattle as far away as Scotland. But here's the thing: It's a *happy* noise. These girls are the happiest people I know. *Everything* makes them laugh. They love *everything*, except the things they hate, and they love hating those things. They literally cannot contain their happiness: It explodes from them constantly in shrieks and shouts, enveloping them in a loud cloud of pure joy. It gets even louder when the radio plays their favorite song—which is basically every song—and they all sing joyfully along at the top of their lungs. For example, recently, as I was driving them to practice, the girls—most of these are good Catholic girls who attend Catholic school, where they receive religious instruction—suddenly, in unison, began belting out these lyrics:

> *My anaconda don't want none unless you GOT*
> *BUNS, HON!*

This is the chorus to a song called "Anaconda," in which a man—Sir Mix-a-Lot—is declaring his fondness for large buttocks on women. The "anaconda" refers to one of his body parts. (Hint: Not his pancreas.)

I know what you're thinking: Why did I let the girls listen to such an inappropriate song? Why didn't I change the station? My excuses are:

1. It took me a while to figure out that the song was not about an actual anaconda.

2. If I changed the station, odds are that the new station would also be playing "Anaconda," or another song that was just as inappropriate. As far as I can tell from driving the car pool, all radio stations play the same two inappropriate songs in heavy rotation.

3. Young people have been listening to inappropriate songs on the radio for centuries, dating back to when I was a young person and we listened to "Louie Louie," which everybody knew had dirty words, although nobody knew exactly what they were:

Louie Louie
[Something unintelligible but supposedly
  obscene]
Yi yi yi yi!

But getting back to happiness: I envy my daughter and her friends. I wish I could be as happy as they are, although I wouldn't want to have to go back to high school and deal with acne and the cosine again. I want to be happy AND be a grown-up, if that's possible. But as I say, happiness is elusive.

Which brings us to this book. It's a group of essays on a variety of topics. They may seem pretty random, but in fact there's an underlying theme, which is happiness. There's an essay about my parents' generation, which I believe somehow managed to be happier than mine, which was *not* supposed to happen. There's a letter to my grandson, imparting wisdom that I hope will enable him to have a happy and fulfilling life, or at least keep him from unnecessarily refrigerating his condiments. There's an essay on whether adopting modern technology—specifically Google Glass—can bring happiness (SPOILER ALERT: No). There's an essay on the never-ending funfest that is cable TV news, and one on David Beckham, who makes many people happy, but not me. There are reports on my trips to Brazil, which is basically a happy place, and Russia, which might be, but I had no idea what anybody was saying. There's some advice for my daughter as she reaches the age when she can legally drive in Florida, which makes her happy, although it terrifies me. And there's an essay on home ownership, which is the American dream, and a guaranteed way to not achieve happiness.

So that's the book. I hope you like it. I hope it makes you happy.

If not, there's always beer.

BITE ME, DAVID BECKHAM

* * *

I hate David Beckham. To understand why, take a moment to examine the picture below. It's my yearbook photo from my senior year at Pleasantville (N.Y.) High School, where I was a member of the class of 1965:

This photo has not been retouched. This is what I actually looked like when I was a senior in high school and desperate to be accepted by my peers, or at least not get beaten up by them.

Perhaps you are thinking: "Hey, don't be so hard on yourself! Back then *everybody* looked like a dweeb!"

I appreciate your thoughtful effort to console me, but no, not everybody did. Many people back then looked normal; some were actually quite attractive. I was not one of them, as you can clearly see. Remember: This was my *high school yearbook photo*, which means I was actively trying to look good when it was taken. This was *the best I could do*.

Part of the problem was simple genetics. I was not a naturally good-looking male. Also I was a late developer puberty-wise. In the photo, I'm looking thoughtfully into the distance, as if I'm thinking: "I wonder what the future holds in store as I prepare to depart from high school and enter the next phase of my life." In fact I am thinking: "I wonder if I will ever develop body hair."

Speaking of which: Note my haircut. I appear to be wearing a malnourished weasel on my head. How did I achieve that look? I'll tell you how: *My dad cut my hair.* He was a Presbyterian minister. He had received extensive training in theology, but, incredibly, this training did not include a single course in hair design. Also he was bald.

Nevertheless, for years my dad cut my hair, and my brothers' hair, using electric clippers that he bought at a drugstore. In my opinion it is tragic that our elected officials, who are always making such a fuss about assault rifles, make no effort whatsoever to regulate the sale of electric hair clippers to civilians. In a sane world, my dad would never have been allowed to possess those things. He was a thoughtful, wise and kind man, but he had the hairstyling talents of an enraged barn owl. Consider, for example, this sector of my haircut:

What are we to make of these two strange, vaguely claw-like hair formations on my forehead? It's not at all clear what their role in the hairstyle is. Are they supposed to belong to the majority of my hair, drifting off to the side? Or are they supposed to be pointing down and forming bangs? Apparently they cannot decide! So they're just going to loiter there in the middle of my forehead, looking weird. *In my high school yearbook photo.* Which is the PERMANENT REC-ORD OF WHAT I LOOKED LIKE IN HIGH SCHOOL.

Not that I am bitter.

Now consider my eyeglasses:

I started wearing glasses in third grade. I was the first kid in my class to need them. I was also one of the smaller kids, which made me the Puny Kid With Glasses, often sensitively referred to by the other kids* as "Four-Eyes." My mom took me to get my glasses at the optical department of Macy's in White Plains, N.Y., which offered basically one style of eyeglasses for boys, which should have been called "You Will Die a Virgin."

Today, 1960s-style eyeglass frames are considered "retro" and are worn ironically by members of the hipster community. Ha-ha! How clever of you, hipsters! Maybe, to complete the "look," you can also develop a case of retro 1960s-style acne, causing zits the size of hockey pucks to erupt randomly

---

*You know who you are.

on your face, especially on those rare occasions when you had the opportunity to talk to an actual girl. Wouldn't that be *ironic*?!

Not that I am bitter about that, either.

Anyway, my point is that in high school I was not physically attractive to the opposite sex, namely girls.

"But Dave," I hear you remarking, "looks aren't everything! There are plenty of other qualities besides cuteness that girls look for in boys."

Good point! And when I say "Good point!" I mean you are a stupid idiot. The girls of Pleasantville High School were not interested in "plenty of other qualities besides cuteness." I know this because I HAD plenty of other qualities besides cuteness. Sarcasm, for example. I had a black belt in sarcasm. I went entire *years* without ever saying anything that was not basically the opposite of what I actually thought. Also I could make realistic farting sounds with my hands. These are just two of the many qualities other than cuteness I had in high school. None of them impressed girls. You will never hear a high school girl say about a boy, in a dreamy voice, "He's *so* sarcastic!"

Here is an actual thing that happened to me in eleventh grade:

There was this girl I liked a lot, so I finally worked up the courage to ask her to go with me to the Halloween dance. Incredibly, she agreed, which meant I had an *actual date*. And it was a magical date indeed, right up until the moment when, as my date and I stood side by side watching people dance in the Pleasantville High gym, I happened to glance over to the *other* side of my date and saw that *she was holding hands with another boy*. Yes. Talk about an awkward moment! Talk about a long, horrendously uncomfortable ride home! Fortunately, I have totally gotten over this incident, and the hideous humiliating memory of it has not festered in my brain ever since, popping up unexpectedly at random moments to torment me like that alien creature that chased Sigourney Weaver around the spaceship. I'm over it! I'M TOTALLY OVER IT, YOU UNDERSTAND??

SO TO SUMMARIZE:

1. In my crucial formative adolescent years, girls liked boys who were cute.
2. I was not cute.
3. I am not at all bitter.

As far as I could tell, the only other quality, aside from cuteness, that girls found attractive in boys was athleticism. Guys who were good at sports, even if they were not cute, were a very big deal at Pleasantville High. In football season we had these Friday pep rallies where the entire student body would gather in front of the school at lunchtime and show their school spirit by sneaking off and smoking cigarettes.

No, that was only a small group of juvenile delinquents.* The rest of the student body participated in cheers led by the PHS cheerleading squad, made up of peppy, attractive, popular girls who would have gone to the prom with a bag full of live tapeworms before they would have gone to the prom with me. This is another thing that I am not at all bitter about.

At the pep rallies, the football players stood on the front steps of the school wearing their varsity letter jackets and looking manly, while we civilian students urged them to fight, fight, fight for the Green and White. I would have *killed* to be standing on the steps wearing a varsity jacket and basking in the adoration of the student body, but I was not football player material. I was more the puny-kid-in-ugly-glasses-who-the-football-players-stuffed-into-the-trash-can-for-amusement material.

I was never good at sports. For a while I played Little

---

*You know who you are.

League baseball, but I had very little interaction with the actual ball. I heard a lot of *yelling* about the ball, and I occasionally sensed that something—which I assumed was the ball—had just whizzed past me. But I almost never had any direct personal *contact* with the ball, which turns out to be crucial to succeeding in many athletic endeavors.

I was like that in every sport. I was not good at catching things or throwing things or even necessarily seeing things. I was not strong, and I could not run particularly fast. My main physical skill was wincing.

Nevertheless, at Pleasantville High I was so desperate to get a varsity letter and be adored by the student body, especially the girl members, that I went out for the track team. My thinking was that since there were many different events in track, I might find one that I was good enough at to get a letter. The event I finally settled on was the long jump, which seemed like a good candidate for me because it involved relatively little actual physical activity. You ran down a short runway, and when you reached this board, you launched yourself into the air, then you landed in a sawdust-filled pit. I figured, how hard could that be?

What I did not anticipate was gravity. Apparently some people contain more gravity than others, and it turned out that for a high school student, I had an extremely high level of gravitational attraction. I was probably affecting the tides. During track team practice I would run down the runway and launch myself from the board, then I would soar through the air for approximately the length of a standard matchbook cover before thudding back to Earth. *Sometimes I couldn't even jump far enough to land in the sawdust pit.* I possessed essentially the same natural leaping ability as the Lincoln Memorial. As a result I took a lot of good-natured ribbing from my fellow track team members. ("You suck." "Why are you even on the track team?" "Who cuts your hair, an enraged barn owl?")

So that was a discouraging time for me. But there's an old saying among jockstraps: "When the going gets tough, the tough get going." These words are very true. Sometimes, when we face adversity, instead of becoming discouraged, we decide to work harder, to show the doubters that they were wrong. This was not one of those times. The doubters were 100 percent correct: I sucked. So I quit the track team. The only way I will ever own a varsity letter is if I buy one on eBay.

(On a more positive note: I *was* elected Class Clown by the Pleasantville High Class of 1965. But that was not much consolation. Another thing you will never hear a high school girl say is, "When I lose my virginity, I want it to be with the Class Clown!")

At this point I hear you saying, "But Dave, so *what* if you were an unattractive, non-athletic, four-eyed, hand-farting loser with zits and a bad haircut in high school? That was many decades ago! Since then you have gone on to enjoy unparalleled success as a minor humor celebrity. You have also made many friends, and apparently even had sexual relations with the opposite sex at least twice. Get over the past!"

Ha-ha! That's easy for you to say, because, as we have already established, you are a stupid idiot. The truth is, I will *never* get over high school. My self-image was permanently etched into my brain back then, and nothing that happened since has changed it. No matter how old I get, when I look in the mirror, this is what I see:

My point—and I admit this is pathetic—is that I am still insecure about how I look. *Deeply* insecure. And this insecurity gets much worse when there are good-looking, athletic guys around.

Which brings us to David Beckham. He is of course the world-famous former soccer star and underwear model who is considered to be the hottest man on Earth by essentially every woman on Earth, a group that unfortunately includes my wife, Michelle. I am not saying Michelle does not love me. What I'm saying is, when she says the words "David Beckham," she gets a certain look on her face that she does not get when she says other words, such as "delicatessen."

"But Dave," I hear you saying, because you apparently are unable to help yourself, "it's perfectly normal for a woman to harbor a harmless 'crush' on a handsome international superstar! It's not as though anything could ever come of it! How would your wife ever even have the opportunity to *meet* David Beckham?"

If you will be quiet for just a moment, I will tell you how. Michelle is a sportswriter. For her entire career, she has been going into locker rooms filled with large athletic naked men who are not wearing any clothes because—as I may have mentioned earlier—they are naked. I can live with that. My wife always tells me that she finds this situation to be very uncomfortable, and I believe her. I'm sure that if I were to walk into a room filled with athletic naked women, I would also be very uncomfortable, although in my case this would be because my eyeballs had fallen out of my head and rolled across the floor from staring so hard.

But here's the problem: One of the sports my wife covers is soccer. It happens that there is a business group seeking to bring a Major League Soccer team to Miami and build a stadium here. It further happens that the leader of that group—as you have probably guessed—is none other than: Danny DeVito.

No, that's who I *wish* were leading the group. But of course it has to be David Freaking Beckham. As I write these words, he has spent the last few months ardently wooing Miami. Every time you turn on the TV, there's David Beckham in Woo Mode, attending government functions, meeting with civic groups, talking with students, rescuing babies from alligators, stopping hurricanes with his bare hands and just generally being handsome and charming and hugely popular in the greater Miami area.

This wooing process included a big downtown reception, to which Michelle, as the *Miami Herald*'s soccer writer, was invited. The good news was, she couldn't attend, because she was at the Sochi Olympics. The bad news was, she arranged invitations for me and our fourteen-year-old daughter, Sophie. Michelle thought it would be, quote, "fun" for Sophie to meet Beckham. That's right: *My wife deliberately arranged for her own daughter, who is female, to physically meet the world's leading sex symbol.*

So Sophie and I went to the reception. Many Miami dignitaries were there, including the mayor, and everybody was very excited. I knew this because people actually got there early, which *never* happens in Miami. This is a Latin town, and we operate on Latin time. If you're invited to, say, a July Fourth picnic scheduled to start at noon, you are considered on time if you arrive any time before Thanksgiving. Miami people are late to their own *funerals.*

But everybody arrived early for the reception. We stood around for twenty minutes in a fairly dignified manner. Then David Beckham came through the door, wearing a suit, and suddenly the dignitaries turned into a mob, swarming toward him as if he were the last lifeboat on the *Titanic.* I've never seen anything like it—all these alleged adults acting like teenage girls, desperately wanting to get next to Beckham, be photographed with him, touch him, and ideally bear his children. And those were the *men.* The women were even more aggressive.

Among those swarming toward Beckham was Sophie,

who managed to get next to him for a photo. I am also in this photo, sort of:

© Seth Browarnik/WorldRedEye.com

That's me, off to the left. I'm the one Sophie is clearly not even vaguely aware of. She wouldn't have noticed if I had been actively on fire. She is totally focused on David Beckham, Hottest Man on the Planet, who has his arm around her, causing her to beam with a look of ecstatic radiant happiness that I will never cause to appear on a female face.

Not that I am bitter!

In the photo I'm smiling, too, because that's what you do when your picture is being taken. Also I was happy for Sophie, because this was a big deal for her. But the truth is, when I look at that photo, this is what I see:

"But Dave," I hear you saying because you will NOT SHUT UP, "so what if your daughter was thrilled by the opportunity to meet this handsome, charming international superstar with a much nicer suit than yours? At least your wife was safely in Russia and thus wasn't there to be swept off her feet!"

No, that happened a couple of weeks later. After Michelle got back from Russia she received an email from one of David Beckham's public relations people about setting up a meeting between him and Michelle. The email contained the following statement, which I am not making up:

> I think David Beckham was thinking of a one-on-one with you, either in a small Herald conference room or your cubicle.

Yes! *David Beckham was thinking of a one-on-one with my wife!* Just the two of them, in her cubicle or a small conference room!

Needless to say, this email generated much excited discussion among my wife's female friends, all of whom voted for the small conference room. They also had many non-journalistic suggestions concerning pedicures, body waxing, etc.

For her part, Michelle, who knows I am deeply insecure, handled the whole thing very sensitively. She assured me that the meeting was going to be just another routine interview for her, although she did not explain why she wore a low-cut strapless evening gown.

No, really, she wore regular business attire to her meeting with Beckham, and when she got back she told me that it had been a strictly professional business encounter and, in all honesty, no big deal. She was obviously lying, but I appreciated the effort.

Anyway, that's why I hate David Beckham. I know it's not his fault that he looks the way he does. I just wish he would go look that way in some other city. But as it stands now, he's going to be around Miami for years, and if I'm not careful, it's going to drive me crazy. I've given a lot of thought to what I should do about this, and I think the time has come for me, finally, to grow up—to get past my juvenile self-image hang-ups; to confront and overcome my insecurity; to stop obsessing pathetically over what I am not and instead learn to accept myself for who I *am*, which is plenty good enough.

So I've made up my mind.

I'm going out for the track team.

A LETTER TO MY DAUGHTER AS SHE BECOMES ELIGIBLE FOR A FLORIDA LEARNER'S PERMIT

✳ ✳ ✳

Unless I Can Get the Law Changed

Dear Sophie—

So you're about to start driving! How exciting! I'm going to kill myself.

Sorry, I'm flashing back to when your big brother, Rob, started driving. You and I both love Rob very much, and he has matured into a thoughtful and responsible person. But when he turned sixteen and got his driver's license, he had a marked tendency to—there is no diplomatic way to put this—drive into things.

This was never his fault. I know this because whenever he drove the car into something, which was every few days, he would call me, and the conversation would go like this:

ME: Hello?

ROB: Dad, it wasn't my fault. ·

Usually what he had driven into through no fault of his own was the rear end of another car. Cars were always stopping unexpectedly in front of Rob for no reason whatsoever. Or possibly—we cannot rule it out—these cars were suddenly materializing from hyperspace directly in front of Rob, leaving him with no option but to run into them. Whatever the cause, it stopped happening when he got older and more experienced and started buying his own insurance.

My point, Sophie, is that just because the State of Florida thinks you can drive a car, that doesn't mean you actually can drive a car. As far as I can tell, after three decades on the roads of Florida, there isn't anybody that the Florida Department of Motor Vehicles *doesn't* think can drive a car. I cannot imagine what you would have to do to fail the driving test here.

DMV OFFICER: OK, make a left turn here.

TEST TAKER: Whoops.

DMV OFFICER: (*Writes something on clipboard.*)

TEST TAKER: Does that mean I fail the test?

DMV OFFICER: Nah, she's getting back up. You
just clipped her.

You may think I'm exaggerating the badness of the drivers down here, Sophie, but that's because you haven't been
at the wheel of a car on the Palmetto Expressway going
60 miles per hour, traveling forward—which, as you will
learn, is considered to be the traditional direction for ve-
hicular traffic on expressways—only to encounter a vehicle,
undoubtedly operated by a licensed Florida driver, going
backward. And not on the shoulder, either. *In your lane.*
This has happened to me more than once; it's how some
Miami drivers handle the baffling problem of what to do
when you miss an exit. When ESPN shows a NASCAR high-
light in which drivers collide at 150 miles per hour and a
dozen cars spin out in a whirling mass of flaming wreckage,
my reaction is: "Big deal. They were all going the same direction. Let's see them attempt to drive on the Palmetto
Expressway."

The State of Florida also does not seem to have a problem
issuing licenses to drivers who are very elderly.

Q. How elderly are they?

A. Their first vehicle was a chariot.

I once had an eye exam during which the ophthalmologist was telling me about some of his older patients, who according to him were basically blind. He said: "I ask them, 'How did you get here?' And they tell me they drove. And I tell them, 'You can't drive. You can't *see*.' And they say, 'How else am I supposed to get here?' And I say, 'I don't know, but you can't *drive*, because you can't *see*.' And then they drive home."

I believe him. I once had a short but terrifying ride on the streets of South Florida in the backseat of a car driven by an elderly man. He was a perfectly nice person, but he had basically the same level of visual acuity as a corn dog. So he outsourced the actual *seeing* part of driving to his wife, who sat in the passenger seat and did her best to keep him posted on what was going on out there in the mysterious region beyond the windshield.

"You have a green arrow," she'd say. "Go. Go. I said GO! No! Wait! Stop! STOP!!"

I believe this Seeing Eye wife arrangement is not uncommon among elderly couples on the roads of South Florida. And if you're wondering why, if the wife can see, she doesn't just drive, the answer is: *The man drives.*

So to summarize, Sophie: Many people who lack the judgment and/or physical skills needed to safely microwave a burrito are deemed qualified by the State of Florida to operate a motor vehicle. When you get out on the road, you will be surrounded by terrible drivers. And guess what? *You will be one of them.* Yes, Sophie: You will be a bad driver, and not because you're careless or irresponsible, but because you're a teenager, and it is a physiological fact that at your stage of brain development, you are—to use the term preferred by researchers in the field of neurological science—"stupid."

There is no shame in this. All humans start out stupid, then gradually become more intelligent as they get older (with a few setbacks along the way) until they reach a certain age, after which they start becoming stupider again. Here's a scientific chart illustrating this phenomenon:

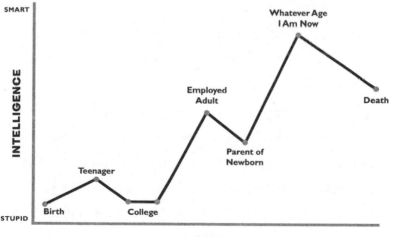

SOURCE: AMERICAN SCIENTIFIC ACADEMY OF SCIENCE

What does this chart tell us, Sophie? It tells us that according to science, even dead people are smarter than teenagers. Teenagers are barely capable of forming sentences. Allowing them to drive—especially if they are males—is insane.

"But Dad," you're thinking, "didn't you drive when you were a teenage male?"

Yes I did. I got my New York State driver's license in 1963, at age sixteen, and I spent many hours cruising on the highways and byways and occasionally the lawns in and around Armonk, N.Y. But that was different, Sophie, because I drove safely. I don't mean "safely" in the sense of "carefully." I was definitely your standard male teenage idiot. But I was a *safe* idiot, because I was driving the safest vehicle ever built: my mom's 1961 Plymouth Valiant station wagon. It did not have modern safety features such as seat belts, air bags, antilock brakes or a computerized collision-avoidance system. What the Valiant had, which was better than any modern technology, was: *Inertia*. I would stomp violently down on the accelerator and basically nothing would happen for several lunar cycles, because the Valiant was no more capable of acceleration than a fire hydrant. This was the only car ever manufactured that traveled faster on the assembly line than under its own power.

You could not hit anything in a Valiant. Fully mature trees moved quickly enough to get out of its way. So it couldn't do any damage even with me at the wheel. If I were in charge, today's teenagers would be permitted to drive *only* if they drove Plymouth Valiant station wagons. Also I would require these teenagers to tune the Valiant's AM radio to New York station WINS and listen to the late Murray the K play hit 1963 tunes such as "Da Doo Ron Ron" because THAT WAS MUSIC, DAMMIT.

Unfortunately, Sophie, I am not in charge, which means you're going to be driving on roads teeming with modern high-speed automobiles operated by incompetent idiots such as (no offense) yourself. To prove that you're qualified to do this, the State of Florida will make you take a test based on the information found in the official *Florida Driver's Handbook*. For example, the test may ask you to identify the Florida "standard" speed in business or residential areas. According to the *Handbook*, the "correct" answer, the one you should mark on your test, is 30 miles per hour.

But listen very carefully, Sophie: If you're driving in Miami and do not wish to be the target of small-arms fire, IN THE NAME OF GOD DO NOT GO AT A "STANDARD" SPEED OF 30 MILES PER HOUR. Miami drivers go faster than that in a car wash. Likewise, the *Driver's Handbook* will tell you that if you're approaching a traffic light as it turns yellow, you should attempt to stop. But in Miami, doing that would cause your car to be instantly converted into a large sheet-metal origami sculpture by the seventeen cars immediately behind you.

My point, Sophie, is that there's a big difference between how the *Florida Driver's Handbook* says you should drive and how actual humans drive in Florida, especially South Florida. So to help you understand the mind-set you will encounter on the roads here, I've prepared this:

REALITY-BASED FLORIDA DRIVER'S Q & A

Q. If I arrive at an intersection at the same time as another motorist, who goes first?

A. You do.

Q. But what if . . .

A. There IS no "what if." YOU GO FIRST.

Q. Florida law strictly prohibits texting while driving. Does this law apply to me?

A. Ha-ha! Of course not.

Q. *If I stop at a red light, how will I know when it turns green?*

A. **You will hear honking behind you. This is your cue to start wrapping up your current text, unless of course it is important.**

Q. *I have noticed that some roads have more than one lane. What is the purpose of the extra lanes?*

A. **To provide a place for you to swerve into while texting.**

Q. *When I come to a stop sign, do I need to stop?*

A. **You personally?**

Q. *Yes.*

A. **No.**

Q. *How is the turn signal used in Florida?*

A. **It is used to indicate to other motorists that you do not realize your turn signal is blinking.**

Q. *Could it also be used to signal your intention to turn or change lanes?*

A. **Interesting! Nobody has ever tried that.**

Q. What is the best kind of food to eat while driving?

A. Any food—such as a sandwich, turkey leg, oyster or Ding Dong—that can be eaten one-handed, so you still have a hand free for texting.

Q. What if an emergency situation arises that might require me to operate the steering wheel?

A. Use your forehead to honk the horn until the emergency has passed.

Q. My car's engine seems to have stopped and I hear a "burbling" noise. What could be causing this?

A. Are you a senior citizen?

Q. Yes.

A. You have driven into a swimming pool.

Q. I am a young male idiot who prefers to drive at a high rate of speed in densely populated areas while texting. How loud should my sound system be?

A. It should emit individual bass notes capable of killing a dog at 50 yards.

Q. *I'm a middle-aged male, and I like to put on skintight, junk-displaying Lycra® cycling shorts and a skintight Lycra® cycling jersey covered with logos for corporations that don't actually pay me anything, then ride around with a large clot of other middle-aged pretend racers screwing up traffic. I don't have a question about driving, but I HAVE JUST AS MUCH RIGHT TO BE IN THIS Q & A AS ANYONE ELSE.*

A. **Everyone hates you.**

Q. *I've had a few drinks. How can I tell if I should drive?*

A. **Take this simple test: Are you wearing your underpants on your head?**

Q. *Not MY underpants, no.*

A. **Then you are good to go.**

Q. *What is all that shouting?*

A. **Are you a senior citizen?**

Q. *Yes.*

A. **You have struck a pedestrian.**

Sophie, I know you think your old man is just kidding. I am not. Ask anybody who drives here: This Q & A reflects the actual situation on the roads of Florida far more accurately than the so-called *Florida Driver's Handbook*. But I didn't write this letter to make you nervous about driving here. I wrote it to make you *terrified* about driving here. Because I love you a lot, and I don't want anything bad to happen to you. I will do everything I can to make sure you're really ready to drive. I'm going to keep coaching you until the day you finally get your license and are allowed to drive alone. Even then, as you leave our driveway, I'll be standing next to the car, giving you last-minute instructions. When you finally drive away, solo at last, you're going to feel as if I'm still right there next to you, guiding you.

In fact I *will* be right there next to you, walking at a leisurely pace alongside your car.

Your 1961 Valiant.

THE REAL
MAD MEN

✳ ✳ ✳

Looking back, I think my parents had more fun than I did.

That's not how it was supposed to be. My parents belonged to the Greatest Generation; they grew up in hard times. My mom was born in Colorado in an actual sod hut, which is the kind of structure you see in old black-and-white photographs featuring poor, gaunt, prairie-dwelling people standing in front of what is either a small house or a large cow pie, staring grimly at the camera with the look of people who are thinking that their only hope of survival might be to eat the photographer. A sod hut is basically a house made out of compressed dirt. If you were to thoroughly vacuum one, it would cease to exist.

My mom, like my dad, and millions of other members of

the Greatest Generation, had to contend with real adversity: the Great Depression, the Dust Bowl, hunger, poverty, disease, World War II, extremely low-fi 78 rpm records and telephones that—incredible as it sounds today—*could not even shoot video.*

They managed to overcome those hardships and take America to unprecedented levels of productivity and power, which is why they truly are a great generation. But they aren't generally considered to be a *fun* generation. That was supposed to be their children—my generation, the Baby Boomers.

We grew up in a far easier time, a time when sod was strictly for lawns. We came of age in the sixties and seventies, the era of sex, drugs and rock and roll. We were cool, we were hip, we were *groovy,* man. We mocked the suit-wearing Establishment squares grubbing for money in their 9-to-5 jobs. That was not for us. We did our *own thing,* you dig? We raised our consciousness. We tuned in, turned on and dropped out. We lived in communes. We went to Woodstock. We had strobe lights and lava lamps. We wore bell-bottom trousers, and *we did not wear them ironically.*

And we had fun. At least I did. I am thinking here of my college and immediate post-college years, when my main goal in life—a much higher priority than academics, or a career—was to have fun. I'm not talking about "fun" in the sense of playing charades, or canoeing. I'm talking about a more hard-core kind of fun, the kind where you might end your night under arrest in an entirely different area code from your underwear. I'm talking about *partying*.

I am also of course talking about alcohol and recreational drugs. So to avoid creating the impression that I am condoning the abuse of these substances, let me clarify, right up front, my views on alcohol and recreational drugs: They are a *lot* of fun.

No! I'm kidding!

Sort of.

What I mean is: Yes, alcohol (which I still consume) (in moderation) (usually) and recreational drugs (which I don't) (although I used to) (but I did not inhale) can be very bad. But they can also, under certain circumstances, be enjoyable, and even sometimes result in high-quality entertainment.

I am not going to name any names here, but back in the seventies, at the wedding reception for Rob and Helene Stavis, I saw my attorney and oldest friend, Joe DiGiacinto, wearing a suit and dress shoes, wade into a large outdoor decorative fountain and attack a statue of the Virgin Mary. It wasn't clear—it still isn't clear—what the statue had done to provoke Joe, but he was really, *really* pissed off at it. The result was a highly entertaining battle, Joe vs. the Blessed Virgin (Joe lost), which remains my fondest memory of any wedding I have ever attended, including my own. It goes without saying that it would never have happened without alcohol.

I myself have been involved in more than a few memorable situations as a result of alcohol consumption. Granted, I have also done some things I now regret. For example, I owe an apology to former vice president Dick Cheney for my behavior at a social function I attended at the *Washington Post* back during the administration of George H. W. Bush, back when Dick was U.S. Secretary of Defense. It was a small affair, maybe two dozen people, and Dick was the guest of honor. After several trips to the bar I somehow got it into my head that it would be hilarious to repeatedly re-introduce myself to him. Every time he turned around—this was in a smallish room—there I was, sticking out my hand and saying, "Hi, Dick! Dave Barry!" Then we would have this awkward handshake, because when somebody sticks his hand out to you, your automatic reaction, even if you are Secretary of Defense, is to stick *your* hand out, only to realize that the person is an intoxicated moron you have already shaken hands with. So that's what I did to Dick. It might have been funny the first four times, but the last two or three were definitely overkill.

I am not proud of my behavior that night. Nor am I proud of those times—there were several—when, as a guest at a party in somebody's home, I set off bottle rockets indoors (although, in my defense, some of those were return fire). I also now regret that I once was involved in an evening that began with drinks called "Singapore slings" and ended with an innocent horse being painted red. Granted, we used a water-based paint. But still.

There are other alcohol- or drug-related things I regret doing, things that I prefer not to elaborate on here other than to apologize to all the people who, over the years, for one reason or another, I have thrown up on. But for the most part, I look back fondly on the era when I partied hearty, at least what I remember of it.

That era was basically my twenties. When I got into my thirties, and especially when I became a parent, my concept of "fun" changed, becoming less likely to involve people getting high or hammered or naked, and more likely to involve balloon animals. It was still *fun*, but it was a far more sedate brand of fun.

In time I came to accept it as a normal part of growing up. I hate to generalize,* but I think this is the pattern for

*Not really. I love to generalize.

most people of my generation and those following us: You party hard into your twenties, maybe a little later. But then, as the burdens of age and career and—above all—parenthood press down on you, you put your bong collection on craigslist and settle down. By your mid-thirties your hard-partying days are over. You get serious about the job of parenting. It's the inevitable course of adulthood. It has always been that way.

Or so I used to think.

What changed my mind was *Mad Men*, the widely acclaimed TV series about Madison Avenue in the sixties. One of the things the show is acclaimed for is its authenticity, which is significant because, if the show really is authentic, then people in the advertising industry back then spent roughly 90 percent of their time smoking, drinking or having extramarital sex. Here's a typical *Mad Men* scene:

Don Draper walks into the Madison Avenue advertising agency where he is an executive. He approaches his office. An attractive secretary sits at the desk outside.

LIVE RIGHT AND FIND HAPPINESS

SECRETARY:

Good morning, Mr. Draper.

DRAPER:

Good morning.

They have extramarital sex.

DRAPER:

Hold my calls.

He goes into his office, lights a cigarette, pours himself a glass of whiskey. The intercom buzzes.

DRAPER:

Yes?

SECRETARY (*on intercom*):

Mr. Draper, there's an attractive woman here to see you.

DRAPER:

Is it my wife?

SECRETARY:

No.

DRAPER:

Send her in.

An attractive woman enters the office.

WOMAN:

Hello, Don.

DRAPER:

Hello.

They have extramarital sex.

WOMAN:

Good-bye, Don.

DRAPER:

Good-bye.

She leaves. Draper lights another cigarette and pours himself another glass of whiskey.

LIVE RIGHT AND FIND HAPPINESS

SECRETARY (*on intercom*):
Mr. Draper, some of your fellow
executives are here to talk
to you.

DRAPER:
About what?

SECRETARY:
Advertising.

DRAPER:
Advertising?

SECRETARY:
Yes. You're an advertising
executive.

DRAPER:
Oh right, I forgot. Send them in.

*Several executives enter. Draper
pours them drinks. They all light
cigarettes.*

EXECUTIVE:

Don, we need to sell some
advertising.

DRAPER:

OK. Hey, one of you is a woman.

They have extramarital sex.

And so on. If *Mad Men* really is authentic, it explains much about the TV commercials of my childhood,
which, in terms of intellectual content, make the commercials of today look like *Citizen Kane*. Back then many
commercials featured a Male Authority Figure in the form
of an actor pretending to be a doctor or scientist. Sometimes, to indicate how authoritative he was, he wore a
white lab coat. The Male Authority Figure usually spoke
directly to the camera, sometimes using charts or diagrams
to explain important scientific facts, such as that certain
brands of cigarettes could actually soothe your throat, or
that Anacin could stop *all three* known medical causes of
headaches:

1. Electrical bolts inside your head.
2. A big coiled spring inside your head.
3. A hammer pounding inside your head.

Another standard character in those old commercials, providing contrast to the Male Authority Figure, was the Desperately Insecure Housewife, who was portrayed by an actress in a dress. The Desperately Insecure Housewife was always close to suicide because she had some hideous inadequacy as a homemaker—her coffee was bitter, her laundry detergent was ineffective against stains, her meat loaf failed to excite her family, she had odors emanating from her carpet, etc. She was under tremendous stress. She couldn't even escape to the bathroom without being lectured on commode sanitation by a tiny man rowing a rowboat around inside her toilet tank.

Even back then, everybody thought these commercials were stupid. But it wasn't until years later, when I started watching *Mad Men*, that I realized *why* they were so stupid: The people making them were so drunk they had the brain functionality of road salt.

FIRST AD EXECUTIVE: I got it! We put a tiny man in a rowboat in the toilet tank.

SECOND AD EXECUTIVE: Perfect! Pass the whiskey.

But here's the thing: Despite all the drinking and sex on *Mad Men*, nobody ever seems to have any fun. The characters are almost universally miserable. And that, to me, does not seem authentic.

I grew up during the *Mad Men* era; my family, like many of the *Mad Men* characters, lived in Westchester County, N.Y.—in our case, the village of Armonk. Most of the moms of Armonk back then were housewives; many of the dads— mine was one—rode the train to work in New York City. Some of those dads, including friends of my parents, were advertising executives.

So during my childhood I got to watch a sliver of the *Mad Men* generation as they went through their late twenties, into their thirties and forties, raising their kids, pursuing their careers and, in some cases, becoming very successful. Like the *Mad Men* characters, they smoked a lot and drank a lot, including at work. I don't know how much extramarital sex went on, and I don't want to know.

But I do know this: Unlike the *Mad Men* characters, the grown-ups back then had fun. A *lot* of fun. And it didn't stop just because they had kids. My parents had a large circle of friends, and just about every weekend, throughout my childhood, they had cocktail parties, which rotated from house to house. I *loved* it when the party was at our house. Dozens of cars filled our driveway and lined the narrow dirt road we lived on, and dozens of couples poured into the house— the men in suits and ties, the women in dresses and heels, everybody talking, shouting, laughing, eating hors d'oeuvres, smoking, heading to the lineup of bottles on the kitchen counter to pour another drink.

My sister and brothers and I would lurk on the edges of the party, watching the show, until we got noticed and sent off to bed. But we didn't go to sleep; we'd sneak back and peek into the smoke-clouded living room to watch as the party got more boisterous, the sound rising to a joyous roar. Sometimes the partiers sang, pounding on our upright piano and belting out popular songs, or parody songs they wrote, sometimes on the spot, to celebrate somebody's birthday or some other occasion. They'd give each other elaborate gag gifts, and sometimes put on skits or little musical shows, complete with costumes. They held theme parties—charades parties, talent show parties, parties involving scavenger hunts. They'd hire a dancing instructor to teach them the mambo, the cha-cha, the twist, whatever was popular. The parties would go late into the night; the next morning, the living room would be littered with empty drink glasses, loaded ashtrays and, occasionally, a partier or two snoring on the sofa.

One morning, after my parents had hosted a scavenger hunt party, my little brother, Phil, came into my bedroom and woke me up, shouting, "There's two giant *B*s in the living room!"

"Giant bees?" I said.

These turned out to be two four-foot-high letter *B*s, made of wood and painted gold. They came from IBM signs that had been erected on property owned by the IBM Corp., which was building its world headquarters in Armonk. How, exactly, the giant *B*s ended up in our living room, and whether IBM was aware of their new location, I do not know. What I do know is that it was a hell of a party.

My parents' big-party era continued until about the time I headed off to college. As they got into their fifties, they still had parties, but these were generally smaller, quieter affairs. By then it was the Boomers' time to have fun. And as I said earlier, we *did* have fun.

But not as much fun as the Greatest Generation. And for nowhere near as many years.

Now, before I get to my point,* I need to stipulate some things:

- Smoking cigarettes is bad for you.
- Drinking too much alcohol is bad for you.
- Driving under the influence of alcohol is very wrong and you should never, ever do it.
- It is also wrong to steal private property from corporations, *even for a scavenger hunt.*
- My parents and their friends probably would have lived longer if their lifestyle choices had been healthier.

So I am conceding that by the standards of today, my parents' behavior would be considered irresponsible. Actually, "irresponsible" is not a strong enough word. By the standards of today, my parents and their friends were crazy. A great many activities they considered to be perfectly OK—hitchhiking, for example; or driving without seat belts; or letting a child go trick-or-treating without a watchful parent hovering within eight feet, ready to pounce if the child is given a potentially lethal item such as an apple; or engaging

---

*You're thinking, "There's a *point*?"

in any form of recreation more strenuous than belching without wearing a helmet—are now considered to be insanely dangerous. By the standards of today, the main purpose of human life is to eliminate all risk so that human life will last as long as humanly possible, no matter how tedious it gets.

And the list of things we're not supposed to do anymore gets longer all the time. Just today, as I was researching this essay,* I encountered an article on the Internet headlined:

IS YOUR HANDSHAKE AS DANGEROUS AS SMOKING?

The answer, in case you are a complete idiot, is: Of *course* your handshake is as dangerous as smoking. The article explains that handshakes transmit germs, which cause diseases such as MERS. MERS stands for "Middle East Respiratory Syndrome," a fatal disease that may have originated in camels. This is yet another argument, as if we needed one, against shaking hands with camels. But the article suggests that we should consider not shaking hands

---

*I am using the phrase "researching this essay" in the sense of "farting around on the Internet to avoid actually writing this essay."

with *anybody*. (Again, Dick Cheney, if you're reading this: I am truly sorry.)

If you could travel back in time to one of my parents' parties and interrupt the singing to announce to the guests that shaking hands could transmit germs and therefore they should stop doing it, they would laugh so hard they'd drop their cigarettes into their drinks. They were just not as into *worrying* as we are today.

And it wasn't just cigarettes and alcohol they didn't worry about. They also didn't worry that there might be harmful chemicals in the water that they drank *right from the tap*. If they wanted to order a dish at a restaurant—chicken, for example—they didn't interrogate the waiter about what ingredients it was prepared with, or whether the chicken contained steroids or was allowed to range freely or was executed humanely; they just ordered the damn chicken. They didn't worry that if they threw their trash into the wrong receptacle, they were killing baby polar bears and hastening the extinction of the human race. They didn't worry about consuming trans fats, gluten, fructose, and all the other food components now considered so dangerous they could be used to rob a bank ("Give him the money! He's got gluten!").

Above all, they did not worry about providing a perfect,

risk-free environment for their children. They loved us, sure. But they didn't feel obligated to spend every waking minute running interference between us and the world. They were parents, but they were not engaged 24/7 in what we now call "parenting," this all-consuming job we have created, featuring many crucial child-rearing requirements that my parents' generation was blissfully unaware of.

They didn't go to prenatal classes, so they didn't find out all the things that can go wrong when a person has a baby, so they didn't spend months worrying about those things. They just had their babies, and usually it worked out, the way it has for millions of years. They didn't have car seats, so they didn't worry that the car seat they just paid $249 for might lack some feature that the car seat their friends just paid $312 for *does* have. They didn't form "play groups" where they sat around with other new parents watching their babies drool and worrying that their drooling baby was behind some other drooling baby in reaching whatever critical childhood development stage they read about in their thirty-seven parenting handbooks written by experts, each listing hundreds, if not thousands, of things they should worry about.

It would never have occurred to members of my parents'

generation to try to teach a two-year-old to read; they figured that was what school was for. And they didn't obsess for
years over *which* school their kids should attend, because
pretty much everybody's kids went to the local schools,
which pretty much everybody considered to be good enough.
They didn't scheme and connive and nag the school admin-
istrators to make sure their kids got certain teachers; their
kids got who they got, and if they didn't get the best teacher,
hey, that was part of life. The parents didn't hover around
the school keeping an eye on their kids and interfering
whenever they felt their child was not getting the absolute
best whatever. They didn't know every grade their child got
on every test. They found out how their child was doing
when the child brought home a report card. If the grades
were bad, they didn't march into the school and complain
that the school had failed their child. They told their child to
shape up, and they maybe even—prepare to be horrified—
gave their child a smack on the back of the head. They didn't
worry that this would scar the child psychologically for life.

They didn't worry that their children would get bored, so
they didn't schedule endless after-school activities and drive
their kids to the activities and stand around with other parents watching their kids engage in the activities. Instead,

they sent their kids out to play. They didn't worry about how or where they played as long as they got home for dinner, which was very likely to involve gluten.

If a kid played a sport, the parents *might* go to the games. But they didn't complain to the coach that their kid wasn't playing enough, or make fools of themselves by getting into fights with other parents or screaming at the referee. It just wasn't that big a deal to them. It was kids playing games.

I'm not saying my parents' generation didn't give a crap. I'm saying they gave a crap mainly about big things, like providing food and shelter, and avoiding nuclear war. They'd made it through some rough times, and now, heading into middle age, building careers and raising families, they figured they had it pretty good. Not *perfect*, but pretty good. So at the end of the workweek, they allowed themselves to cut loose—to celebrate their lives, their friendships, their success. They sent the kids off to bed, and they partied. They drank, laughed, danced, sang, maybe stole a piece of an IBM sign. They had fun, *grown-up* fun, and they didn't feel guilty about it.

Whereas we modern parents, living in the era of Death by Handshake, rarely pause to celebrate the way our parents did because we're too busy parenting. We never *stop* parenting. We are *all over* our kids' lives—making sure they get whatever they want, removing obstacles from their path, solving their problems and—above all—worrying about what else will go wrong, so we can fix it for them. We're in permanent trick-or-treat mode, always hovering eight feet away from our children, always ready to pounce on the apple.

Yes, we've gotten really, really good at parenting, we Boomers. This is fortunate, because for some inexplicable reason a lot of our kids seem to have trouble getting a foothold in adult life, which is why so many of them are still living with us at age thirty-seven.

They're lucky they have us around.

IN WHICH WE LEARN TO LOVE BRAZIL, AND TRY TO HATE BELGIUM

✳ ✳ ✳

When I told people I was going to Brazil, they all had basi-cally the same reaction:

"Brazil is a beautiful country!" they'd say. "Don't wear any jewelry!"

Or: "The Brazilians are so nice! Do NOT carry cash!"

And so on. It was always some form of "It's going to be great!" followed by "You're going to die."

The guidebooks had basically the same message: Lavish praise for the beauty of Brazil and its warmhearted people, sprinkled with warnings not to carry your passport, never to display your phone in public, not to carry too much money, not to leave the airport, etc. There was also advice on what to do when—inevitably—you got robbed: You were to hand over your money immediately when the robbers showed you their knife, which apparently was the standard Brazilian street robbery procedure. Some experts recommended that you carry two wallets, or keep your money in separate wads, so that you could give money to the robbers and still have some left.

I'll be honest: These warnings made me nervous. This is pretty funny when you consider that I live in Miami, which can be a dangerous place, with a segment of the population capable of horrific acts of violence. And those are the *police*. The criminals are even worse.

So you'd think I wouldn't be afraid of mere knife-wielding Brazilian street robbers. But I was. To prepare for the trip, I purchased a variety of robber-thwarting items, including shorts and shirts that had secret pockets, and several hidden pouch things that you attach to your belt and wear inside your pants, thus rendering your valuables invisible, as well as, on a hot day, too disgusting to steal.

Perhaps you're wondering why, if I was so worried, I didn't just cancel my trip, or go someplace that seemed safer than Brazil, such as Afghanistan. The answer is that Brazil was hosting the World Cup, the biggest soccer tournament of all. My sportswriter wife Michelle, who has covered six

World Cups, was going to be in Brazil for five weeks, and the plan was for me and our daughter Sophie to go down and spend some time with her.

But there was another reason I wanted to go: I have become a big fan of the World Cup and the sport of soccer. This is a fairly recent development in my life. Like most Americans my age (107), I grew up in an era when, if you were a boy, you played the traditional American sports: baseball, football, basketball, farting and throwing rocks at your friends. In gym class, we sometimes engaged in an activity called "soccer," but I am putting it in quotation marks because you couldn't really call what we did an actual sport. We did not care, at all, who won. We basically stood around on the field in random semi-motionless clots. If the ball happened to roll into our immediate vicinity, we kicked it, but our objective was to send it into somebody else's vicinity so that we would no longer have to concern ourselves with it. It never occurred to us to try to use the ball to achieve some larger purpose.

In college, during the sixties, I played intramural soccer, but again, it was not highly competitive. Our sole athletic objective, as players, was to fulfill the college athletic requirement. So the mood tended to be very mellow.

Q. *How mellow was it?*

A. I once smoked a joint on the field *during a game*.

After college I pretty much forgot about soccer for several decades. I was vaguely aware that abroad it was popular to the point of fatal riots. But I never watched international soccer.

This changed in 1998 thanks to my wife, who went to France when it hosted the World Cup. My son Rob and I joined her in Paris for the last three weeks of the tournament. It turned out to be the best party I ever attended. I've been to Super Bowls, World Series and the Olympics; I've been part of vast boisterous, barfing mobs in Times Square and Bourbon Street. But I'd never seen anything like the summer of 1998 in Paris. The streets were packed with happy, face-painted, flag-draped fans from all over the world, singing, dancing, chanting, mooning* and making a valiant effort to consume all the alcohol in Western Europe. These people had *unbelievable* partying stamina. They went hard all night, every night. I'm sure most of them died soon

---

*I refer here to the Scots, who, it turns out, are not in fact wearing anything under those kilts. They are *hard-core* partiers. If the World Cup were a drinking competition, Scotland would always finish first, as well as second through tenth.

afterward from bodily abuse. But they had a LOT of fun while they lasted.

Another wonderful aspect of that World Cup was seeing the French undergo a transformation from a people who were too reserved, sophisticated, intellectual and just generally French to concern themselves with some childish game into batshit soccer maniacs. The French team that year was not favored to win, or even do particularly well; when Rob and I arrived, the locals we spoke to generally sneered at all the rah-rah patriotism of the foreign fans. The sneering began with the taxi driver who drove us from the airport, who, having determined that we were Americans and therefore yahoos, said, "To you, *ze sport* is very important. We do not care so much about *ze sport*."

We heard a lot of that. But the French team kept winning, and with each win the French people found that they cared more about *ze sport*. By the time they got into the final, everybody in Paris, including the *Mona Lisa*, was wearing blue, white and red face paint. In the final game, France played Brazil, which was heavily favored. But the French team—led by a wondrously talented player with the wondrous name Zinedine "Zizou" Zidane—won, and Paris went completely insane.

Rob and I were among the million or so beyond-ecstatic

people celebrating on the Champs-Élysées that night, and random French persons kept hugging and even kissing us, despite the fact that we were American yahoos. It was such a wildly happy night that the devastated Brazilians—there were thousands in Paris—soon ceased despairing about their loss and commenced partying. (The Brazilians are party people; more on this later.)

But it wasn't just the partying that got me into the World Cup; it was also—in fact mainly—the sport of soccer. I had never seen it played at the world-class level. All of the soccer I'd watched, aside from the pathetic school games I'd played in, involved my kids playing what we Americans call "youth soccer." I am not knocking youth soccer. It's a wholesome family activity that involves a tremendous amount of family togetherness in the form of families spending a lot of time together in confined spaces such as cars. There is so much togetherness that sometimes you sincerely want, as a family, to strangle each other.

My daughter Sophie plays on a "travel" team, which means that every weekend we travel approximately 200 miles to play in a tournament against other travel teams, which have also traveled long distances, sometimes coming from the very same city where we originated. The reason we travel these distances, rather than just stay home and play each other there, is that the games must be played in a place where there is a reasonable chance that somebody will be struck by lightning. All youth soccer tournaments—this is a strict rule—must be played in a locale with a 95 percent or greater probability of violent thunderstorms. If we truly want to end the drought in sub-Saharan Africa, all we have to do is schedule a youth soccer tournament there. The entire region will be underwater within hours.

So our youth soccer experience involves spending many hours in parking lots during heavy downpours, huddled together, as a family, in our cars, waiting for lightning to stop striking the field. On those rare occasions when the weather permits the girls to play, the parents, most of whom could not personally kick a ball without spraining both ankles, stand on the sidelines and yell contradictory instructions—"Go to the ball!" "Spread out!" etc.—which the girls wisely ignore. Every now and then one of the teams scores a goal, at which point all the parents of the opposing team yell, "Offside!" Offside is an important soccer rule that nobody really understands, so everybody yells it a lot. When the tournament ends, the parents experience either the thrill of victory or the agony of defeat, while the girls resume taking selfies.

I enjoy watching Sophie's games, because she is my

daughter and I love her and I would happily watch her peel turnips. But I am frankly not interested in watching youth soccer unless one of the youths playing is my child. Whereas I think that big-time international soccer—the kind I saw for the first time at that 1998 World Cup—is the best sport there is.

I realize that many Americans disagree with me on this. Many Americans think soccer is awful. Among the main criticisms are:

- It's foreign.
- Many foreigners are involved.
- These people call it "football."
- It's not football! *Football* is football.
- You can't even use your hands!
- It's boring.
- Nobody ever scores.
- If anybody ever *does* score, it doesn't count because he was "offside."
- Whatever the hell THAT means.
- It's SOOOO boring.
- Seriously: *Nobody ever scores.*
- Sometimes the games end in ties.
- TIES, for God's sake.

- Why do they even bother using a ball?
- Despite the fact that nothing ever happens, the fans spend the entire game jumping up and down like prairie dogs on cocaine, while bellowing allegedly clever songs in foreign languages to the tune of "Oh My Darling, Clementine."
- The players are foreign.
- They sport haircuts that were apparently administered by a blind heroin addict in the men's room of a Bulgarian disco in 1978.
- Some of the players use only one name. There are famous Brazilian players named "Fred," "Hulk" and "Kaka."
- *Kaka*, for God's sake.
- Also they are complete wusses. Whenever they collide with something, such as another player, a tall-ish blade of grass or an unusually dense patch of air, they try to draw a foul call by hurling themselves dramatically to the turf, grabbing a random knee—it's always a knee—and adopting the agonized facial expression of a man being castrated by irate lobsters.
- If they don't get the foul call, they're back on their feet seconds later, miraculously healed from their near-fatal pretend injury.

- On those seemingly random occasions when the referee *does* call a foul, *nothing happens.* The players simply resume running around and falling down.

- But sometimes—for what appears to be exactly the same foul—the referee makes a big show of sternly displaying a yellow card to the player, looking not unlike a person brandishing a crucifix at a vampire. When this happens, the result is: Still basically nothing.

- But on certain very special fouls—which, again, often do not appear to the naked eye to be any worse than any of the *other* fouls—the referee shows the player the dreaded Crucifix of Doom red card, and the player receives the most feared punishment in all of soccer: A normal haircut.

- No, seriously, the red-carded player must leave the game, which means his team has to play the rest of the game with fewer players, which means it is *even less likely,* if such a thing is possible, that they will ever score a goal.

- Sometimes the referee squirts a line of what appears to be shaving cream onto the field and the players line up behind it holding their hands protectively over their family jewels, looking like the waiting room at an express vasectomy clinic.

- The scoreboard clock counts *up*, instead of down, as God clearly intended.
- Also, unbelievably, the scoreboard clock *doesn't show the official time.* The official time is a secret known only to the referee, who keeps it on his special referee wristwatch that *nobody can see except him.*
- Also the referee has the power to add some semi-random amount of minutes at the end to compensate for time wasted by players suffering comically fake injuries, which means that in the crucial final minutes of a close game *nobody knows how much time is actually left.* Instead of watching the scoreboard, everybody is watching the referee, who keeps frowning at his wristwatch, like a middle-aged, shorts-wearing commuter whose bus is late.
- And NOBODY EVER SCORES.

These are the main criticisms leveled against soccer by American critics. In response to these critics, I say: Fair enough! You make some excellent points.

Oh, if I wanted to, I could make some counterpoints

regarding popular American professional sports. For example, I could note that if you're watching a baseball game, you can get up pretty much anytime you want and go do something else for a while—use the bathroom; make dinner; obtain a degree from dental school—without missing much action, unless you count players spitting, scratching and adjusting their packages. This is especially true if the game involves a "no-hitter" or a "pitcher's duel," which are special forms of high-voltage baseball excitement in which one or both of the teams never even *threaten* to score.

Or I could note that a great deal of professional football consists of the players huddling—which is essentially holding a meeting—or else just standing around waiting during the many, many time-outs required so that the viewers at home can watch Viagra commercials. Even when a team does run an actual play, most of the time it's a running play for little or no gain, meaning that it lasts about five seconds, during which very little is accomplished other than pretty much everybody on the field falling down. Then it's time for: More meetings! And on those infrequent occasions when a play gains serious yardage, it is typically called back because of "holding," which is an infraction defined as "something that happens on every single freaking football play."

Years ago, when Sophie was two, she watched part of an

NFL game with me. After a few minutes she got the hang of it and started delivering a running commentary, as follows:

> **SOPHIE** (*when the teams lined up*): "Ready."
> **SOPHIE** (*when the ball was snapped*): "Fall down!"

This—"Ready" . . . "Fall down!"—would be a perfectly accurate play-by-play call for much of the action in pro football. The time breakdown of a typical three-hour NFL game broadcast is roughly as follows:

- Actual football plays: 12 minutes.
- Slow-motion replays shown while the teams hold meetings: 43 minutes.
- Close-ups of the backsides of officials peering at a special monitor to review questionable plays: 11 minutes.
- Referees announcing "holding" penalties: 14 minutes.
- Close-ups of cheerleaders smiling maniacally while making that bizarre hand motion wherein they appear to be violently grating cheese with their pom-poms: 7 minutes.
- Viagra commercials: 93 minutes.

And then there is golf. I am not a sadistic person, so I'm not going to note all the things that I could note about golf, except to say that if your idea of excitement is watching men in slacks squat on their haunches, trying to envision which way the little ball will roll when they finally get around to actually hitting it, then you will be very, very excited by golf.

"OK," I hear you soccer critics respond, "what about professional basketball? There's a *lot* of scoring in that sport." Yes, there is. There is so much scoring that any given individual basket tends to be close to meaningless. That is why, as has been noted by many, you can skip the first 46 minutes of any given professional basketball game, secure in the knowledge that with 2 minutes left, the score, unless it is a meaningless game—which is approximately 87 percent of all NBA games—will be approximately 105 to 102, and that it will take roughly an hour to play those last 2 minutes because there will be 29 fouls, 14 time-outs and 37 Viagra commercials.

Am I saying that I don't like these traditional American sports? No!* I'm a traditional American, and I enthusiastically watch, or at least enthusiastically doze on the sofa in front of, all of these sports. I'm not saying they're *bad*; I'm

---

*Seriously: No.

just saying they're stupid. ALL sports are fundamentally stupid. That's why they're popular.

So here are four reasons why I love soccer:

1. *It keeps moving.* There are no time-outs, and (except during halftime) no commercials. This is one of the reasons why the players fake injuries: They're exhausted and looking for a few seconds' rest.

(Just for the record, most soccer fans hate the diving and injury faking. Although it can sometimes be amusing: Some teams have raised it to an art. Not to single out any specific nation, but there are Italian players who spend enough time lying on the ground to be biologically classified as zucchini.)

2. *The skill involved is astounding.* You're watching the offense advance the ball via a series of pinpoint passes, each player knowing before the ball reaches his feet what he plans to do with it the instant it arrives. Suddenly a defensive player, having anticipated a pass, launches himself horizontally feetfirst, makes a sliding tackle and steals the ball, somehow managing to spring back to his feet and control it at the same time. He glances downfield and sends the ball 50 yards through the air, perfectly leading a sprinting teammate, who, outleaping his defender, gets his forehead on the ball and, snapping his head just right, flicks the ball another 20 yards through the air to another sprinting teammate,

who traps the ball with his chest and, before it hits the ground, delicately lofts it over two defenders to a teammate streaking toward the goal, who plants his feet as the ball arrives, leaps high into the air, flips over backward and, with his feet well above his head, executes a bicycle kick, blasting the ball with exquisite accuracy—remember, this guy is *upside down* and using his *foot*—at the upper right-hand corner of the goal, where, at the last possible nanosecond, it is barely—just *barely*—deflected over the bar by the outstretched fingertips of a diving goalie with the reflexes of a *Twilight* vampire.

In other words—and you will see plays like this over and over in high-level soccer—these guys have changed instantly from defending to counterattacking, moving the ball the length of the field in a few seconds via a sequence of amazingly accurate, brilliantly improvised passes leading to a spectacular shot that, thanks to a spectacular defensive play, is unsuccessful.

So, no goal. Nobody ever scores in soccer! It's so boring!

Unless you actually watch it.

This leads me to the quality I love most about soccer, and it's the very quality used most as a criticism:

3. *It's really, really, really hard to score.* The nature of the sport is such that the defense usually has the advantage.

In high-level soccer, where defenders rarely make mistakes, there are few easy goals; most of them range from very difficult to more or less impossible. You might wait an hour for your team to score a goal; you might wait two; it might not happen at all. The tension builds and builds, and becomes almost unbearable as, over and over again, the team *almost* scores, or is *almost* scored upon.

So when a goal finally comes—if it ever does—it feels SO good. Or, bad. Either way, you *feel* it, more intensely than in any other sport I know of. When your team scores in basketball, it's a pleasant feeling, but a short-lived one, like a satisfying burp. When your team scores in soccer, it's an orgasm.

Which brings me to the fourth reason why I love soccer:

4. *Soccer fans are insane.* You really have to sit among them to appreciate how insane they are. The grandstands at a major soccer match make the grandstands at a big-time American college football rivalry game—say, Ohio State vs. Michigan—look like a meeting of the Rotary Club. There is simply no party like a big soccer party, and there is no soccer party bigger than the World Cup. Which is why I wanted to go to Brazil, despite the likelihood that I would not survive.

Getting to Brazil was not easy. It turns out that if you're a U.S. citizen, you need a visa, which is a special piece of paper you must obtain from the Brazilian government via a process clearly designed to prevent you from ever actually obtaining a visa. This seemed stupid to me: I mean, there I was, an American who wanted to go to Brazil and contribute to the economy by staying in hotels, eating at restaurants and getting robbed at knifepoint. Why would the Brazilian government want to make this difficult for me?

The reason, it turns out, is that Brazil is retaliating against the United States, which, for what I'm sure are stupid reasons, requires Brazilians to get visas before they are allowed to come here and help our economy. So this is a case of two nations harming themselves via a strategy of stupidity and counter-stupidity, which is the basis of most international relations. It's only a matter of time before we go to war.

To apply for our visas, we had to go to the Brazilian consulate in Miami, which permits people to submit applications in person between the convenient hours of 10 a.m. and noon on weekdays only. Michelle and I got there early, but there was already a crowd ahead of us, overflowing the small waiting area. There were three service windows, only one of which conveniently featured an actual human being. She was a polite but strict lady whose job was to patiently explain to the people who shuffled forward, one by one, documents in hand, that unfortunately their application was incomplete. Many of these people were making repeat visits to the consulate, but somehow they still didn't have all the items—some of them pretty obscure—that the polite but strict lady required.

> **POLITE BUT STRICT LADY** (*reviewing documents*): I'm sorry, but this is not acceptable.
>
> **VISA APPLICANT:** But yesterday you said . . .
>
> **POLITE BUT STRICT LADY:** I said you needed to provide the original liner notes for the 1965 Dave Clark Five album *Having a Wild Weekend*. These, unfortunately, are the liner notes to another of their 1965 albums, *Weekend in London*.
>
> **VISA APPLICANT:** But this is the sixth time I've been here! Can't you just . . .
>
> **POLITE BUT STRICT LADY:** You will also need to provide the thorax of a juvenile wolverine.

I exaggerate, but only slightly. If the United States ever gets serious about securing the border with Mexico, all we have to do is post this lady down there under a sign that says WELCOME TO THE USA. Nobody will ever get through.

Nevertheless, we eventually managed to get visas, and

the day finally came when Sophie and I flew to Rio de Janeiro (by then Michelle was already in Brazil). We arrived early in the morning and took a taxi to our hotel, which was a little tricky because the taxi driver—I find this to be a recurring problem in foreign countries—did not speak English. Brazilians speak Portuguese, which is somewhat similar to Spanish, as we see in these examples:

ENGLISH	SPANISH	PORTUGUESE
Here is my money.	Aquí está mi dinero.	Aqui está o meu dinheiro.
Please do not stab me.	Por favor, no me apuñalar.	Por favor, não me esfaquear.

I'm not particularly good at languages. The only Portuguese word that really stuck in my brain—don't ask me why—was *borboleta*, which means "butterfly." Fortunately, Sophie speaks Spanish fluently and has a good ear for languages, so she was able to serve as my interpreter in Brazil. With her help, the driver figured out where we wanted to go, and he managed to get us to our hotel without hitting or getting hit by anybody.

This was impressive, because Brazilian drivers view traffic laws as mere suggestions, not meant to constrain a driver who sincerely believes he needs to pass other motorists by driving—we rode in a taxi that did this—on the sidewalk. I rode in another taxi driven by a driver who, as far as I could tell, was not watching the road at all because he was watching a soccer match on a TV screen installed in his dashboard. I didn't say anything, because all I really could have said was *"Borboleta,"* which he might have misinterpreted.

When Sophie and I got to the hotel, we were informed that our room would not be ready for several hours. We decided to pass the time by taking a walk around our neighborhood. This presented a problem, because I was carrying cash, credit cards and passports, all of which I had planned to leave in our hotel room safe to thwart the knifepoint robbers lurking outside the hotel waiting to pounce.

So I went into a men's room and changed into my special anti-robbery, secret compartment shirt and shorts. I also put on *two* secret underpants pouches. I put a small decoy wad of money in an outside pocket to hand over to the robbers, then divided up the rest of my valuables and concealed them in various places on my body. When I lumbered out of the men's room, I was a man of mystery bulges, a human cash piñata. I was also nervous about going outside with Sophie. I had my hand in my pocket, clutching my decoy money wad, ready to throw it at the first Brazilian who got within 10 feet of us.

You probably think I was being ridiculous. But guess what, smarty-pants? Guess what happened to Sophie and me *almost immediately* when we left the safety of the hotel? I'll tell you what: Nothing. Nobody robbed us, at knifepoint or gunpoint or needlepoint or any other kind of point. Nobody paid any particular attention to us at all.

And nothing is what continued to happen to us—that day, and the next day, and the rest of our time in Brazil. Virtually all of the many Brazilians we encountered—and we were not always in nice touristy neighborhoods—were friendly and helpful. Brazil turned out to be one of the most consistently *nice* countries I've ever visited. I wanted to stay longer, and I'll definitely go back. I'm not saying there's no crime in Brazil, or that you shouldn't be careful if you go there. I'm just saying that there's crime everywhere— Washington, D.C., for example—and the threat in Brazil seems to be a tad exaggerated.

My unwarranted nervousness about knifepoint robbers got to be a running joke between me and Sophie. We decided that we could probably make a decent living in Brazil by meeting newly arrived American tourists at the airport and showing them a knife, or even, if they looked especially nervous, a photograph of a knife, maybe even just a receipt for one. Assuming they'd read the same guidebooks I did, they'd hurl money at us and sprint back to their planes.

Anyway, once I relaxed a bit, I started noticing that Rio is a beautiful city, with dramatic mountains popping up scenically all around, and miles of lovely ocean beaches occupied by thousands of mellow Brazilians displaying literally acres of butt cheeks. I refer here to the women of Brazil, who favor very small bathing suits.

Q. How small are they?

A. They look like eye patches for mice.

One standard-size American woman's swimsuit would, if cut into pieces, provide enough fabric to make bathing suits for the entire female population of Rio. And it's not that all the women there are of supermodel caliber; it's just that they don't feel the need to cover much of themselves. I say, God bless them.

Rio is a mellow, casual city. The only men I saw wearing suits and ties were chauffeurs; everybody else seemed to be in flip-flops and T-shirts. The overwhelming majority of the T-shirts, at least while the World Cup was going on, were copies of the yellow jerseys worn by the Brazilian national soccer team. We saw them on everybody—men, women, children, babies, grandparents, store clerks, statues and literally dozens of dogs (Brazilians love dogs).

Everyone says the Brazilians are "passionate" about soccer. This adjective is inadequate. It's like saying the sun is "warm." Many sports fans are passionate. Brazilians are on a different level entirely.

Q. Can you illustrate this point using a particularly gruesome example that is not at all humorous?

A. Yes, but I would prefer not to.

Q. Oh, come on.

A. All right, but remember, this was your idea:

> **In June of 2013, a man named Otávio da Silva was refereeing an amateur soccer match in the northeastern Brazil city of Maranhão. A player named Josemir Santos Abreu committed what Otávio considered to be a foul, so Otávio showed him a red card (this is very bad; see explanation above), thereby ejecting him from the game.**

> **But Abreu refused to leave the field. The two got into a heated altercation, during which Abreu punched Otávio.**

Q. *That isn't so bad! There are plenty of times in American sports when a player and a referee get into . . .*

A. **I'm not done. Otávio, upset about being punched, pulled a knife, and . . .**

Q. *Wait . . . the REFEREE pulled a knife?*

A. **That is correct: The referee in an *amateur soccer match* pulled a knife. He used it to stab Abreu in the chest. Abreu was taken to the hospital, but he died en route.**

Q. *My God! That's horrible!*

A. **Wait. We haven't gotten to the bad part yet.**

Q. *What?*

A. **According to a statement released by the Public Safety Department of the State of Maranhão (as reported by the Associated Press), friends and relatives of Abreu "rushed into the field, stoned the referee to death and quartered his body."**

Q. *They QUARTERED THE REFEREE?*

A. **After stoning him to death, yes. And then . . .**

Q. *THERE'S MORE??*

A. **Unfortunately, yes. According to local news media, the crowd "also decapitated Silva and stuck his head on a stake in the middle of the field."**

Q. *Sweet Lord Jesus.*

A. **Yes. It's on YouTube.**

I want to stress, again, that I always felt perfectly safe when I was in Brazil, and that I found the Brazilian people to be uniformly friendly and welcoming. On any given day, there are probably hundreds, maybe even thousands, of games of soccer played in Brazil, and I'm sure that only a tiny percentage of them end with anybody being quartered. My point in recounting this awful and totally non-humorous incident—which, as you will recall, was your idea—is simply that when it comes to describing how the Brazilians feel about soccer, "passionate" does not get the job done.

During the World Cup, when the Brazilian team was playing, Rio essentially shut down. Most businesses closed; the streets emptied of traffic; the sidewalks were deserted. Every bar and restaurant had TVs tuned to the game, with yellow-shirted crowds spilling out onto the sidewalk. In our hotel, the desk clerks abandoned the desk and went into the bar to watch the game. When Brazil scored a goal, you heard fireworks all around, and a deep, thunderous rumbling roar, seemingly coming from everywhere, from the city itself. When the national team won, the streets flooded with people celebrating. In our neighborhood, the party went on all night; at dawn, people were still singing in the street outside our hotel. This was going on everywhere in Brazil, for every game. This is how big a deal soccer is to Brazilians; this is how proud they are of their team.

Which makes it all the more impressive, the way they reacted when their team was eliminated in spectacularly humiliating fashion, getting obliterated by the Germans, 7–1—an unthinkable score for any World Cup semifinal, let alone one involving Brazil. The Brazilians didn't riot, as some feared they would. They were bummed, of course, but they didn't turn violent, and they didn't plunge into a state of national despair. In fact they managed to find humor in their humiliation, turning to Twitter and other social media to exchange, among other jokes, doctored photos of Rio's giant mountaintop Jesus statue, one with Jesus holding his hands over his eyes. They laughed at themselves.

"What else could we do?" one Brazilian asked me.

"Quarter some Germans" is one answer. But the point is, they didn't.

The German team, which was scarily good and could probably have kicked the ass, using only its feet, of many other nations' actual armies, went on to win the World Cup. Sophie and I saw the German team play the French team in Rio's Maracanã Stadium in front of a highly festive, beer-consuming crowd featuring many people wearing face paint, costumes and—in the case of the French fans—rooster hats.

The rooster, or cockerel, is of course the national symbol of France, and for a very good reason: All the good animals were taken. I mean, let's face it, we are talking about using as the animal representing your country *a male chicken.* Granted, roosters can be fierce, courageous fighters, but that's when their opponents are *other roosters.* They do not fare so well against, for example, dogs, or reasonably large squirrels.

Also the physical format of a rooster frankly does not make for a fear-inducing, warrior-style hat. When you see a French fan coming your way with this fuzzy, plump poultry unit on his head, its feet dangling next to the fan's ears, its head listing sadly to the side, you do not think: "Whoa! This

fan represents a team to be reckoned with!" It did not help that some of the male French fans—and these were not small men—were wearing, in addition to their rooster hats, leotards and tutus. I'm sure they meant this to be self-mockingly funny. And it *was* funny. But still . . .

French fans have been known to release live roosters on the playing field during rugby and soccer matches. This can lead to highly entertaining chases as security personnel try to capture the roosters, which may not be the most fearsome animals but are shifty and can run pretty darned fast. Tragically, no roosters were released in the World Cup match that Sophie and I attended, which may be why France lost, 1–0. Although I believe the tutus were also a factor.

Sophie and I also attended a game between Colombia and Uruguay, which are two countries whose fans, for reasons that are not clear to me, do not like each other. We sat in the middle of a large Colombian rooting section. I had this conversation with the guy sitting next to me:

> **GUY:** Who are you supporting?
> **ME:** Colombia.
> **GUY:** Where are you from?
> **ME:** Miami.
> **GUY:** Miami is almost Colombia.

Which is true. But the reason we were supporting Colombia—aside from the fact that we were surrounded by Colombians—is that the Uruguayans were being obnoxiously defensive about the fact that their star player, Luis Suárez, had been banned from the World Cup following a shocking incident: During a game against Italy, Suárez could clearly be seen on video robbing an Italian player at knifepoint.

No, seriously, Suárez bit Italian defender Giorgio Chiellini. The video (again: YouTube) of this moment is pretty wonderful. Suárez—who had *twice before* gotten in trouble for biting opponents during games—clearly leans over and chomps on Chiellini's shoulder. Chiellini, being a veteran Italian soccer player, immediately falls down. Suárez, for no apparent reason other than that Chiellini has fallen down, also falls down. Chiellini then pulls the neckhole of his jersey down and, yelling to the referee, points to the bite mark on his skin. Suárez, not to be outdone, puts his hands to his mouth and adopts a facial expression indicating great pain, as if to say, "This ruffian has used his shoulder to injure me in the teeth!"

It goes without saying that since an extremely flagrant foul was committed, the referee—this being soccer—did not call a foul on the play. However, upon further review of the video, the authorities booted Suárez from the tournament. This outraged the Uruguayans, who somehow made themselves believe that Suárez—who had clearly (for the *third time*) bitten an opponent in a game televised internationally to millions of viewers—had done nothing wrong, and was in fact the victim. So their fans were in a pissy mood, and it didn't help that fans of opposing teams—the hated Colombians, for example—made great sport of the Suárez incident by wearing vampire teeth, zombie costumes, Hannibal Lecter–style anti-biting muzzles, etc.

Anyway, Colombia won, 2–0, to the rapturous joy of our rooting section. Each time the Colombians scored, the entire team sprinted to a corner of the field and performed, in unison, a well-choreographed and highly entertaining salsa line dance. Also the Colombian fans chanted some uncomplimentary things about Uruguay. As the game wore on, there were several fights in the stands, all of them—according to the Colombians around us—started by Uruguayans.

UNIVERSAL SPORTS FACT: A fight in the stands, no matter how pathetic, is always much more interesting to all of the spectators in the area than anything that is happening on the field.

Sophie and I greatly enjoyed the Colombia–Uruguay and Germany–France games, but the most exciting game for us was the one between the United States and Belgium. It was a round of sixteen game, meaning the winner would advance to the quarterfinals and the loser would be eliminated from the World Cup. So this was our chance to root for our country in a meaningful game.

I began my preparations several days in advance by going to a bar with some other Americans and trying to come up with reasons to hate the Belgians. My goal was to develop a Colombia/Uruguay-style grudge rivalry between us and them. This was not easy. Like most Americans, I don't spend a lot of time thinking about Belgium, and thus there are many things I don't know about it as a country, such as which specific continent it is located on. You don't think of Belgians—at least *I* don't think of Belgians—as being the kind of people who stir up strong passions in others. An expression you almost never hear is: "Those damn Belgians! They're always doing X!" With X representing something unlikable.

But we gave it our best shot, sitting around in the bar. Here are the anti-Belgian ammunition points we came up with:

- The Belgians claim that they, not the French, invented French fries.
- Get over it, Belgium! Nobody cares!
- Also, the Belgians put mayonnaise on their French fries.
- Actually, it might be the Dutch who do that. But the point is, it's *wrong*.
- The Belgians probably did invent Belgian waffles, but why, exactly, do they have to have their own waffles?
- Our waffles aren't good enough for them?

- Hitler was Belgian.
- The Belgians were behind 9/11.

(We came up with those last two ammunition points after several beers, so they might not be 100 percent accurate.)

We also tried to come up with some anti-Belgian chants to chant at the big game. The best we could do were these:

> *Hey, Belgium!*
> *You can go to Hellgium!*

> *You say you invented French fries,*
> *And that's just lies.*

After that the evening got a little murky.

The USA–Belgium game was played in the northern Brazil city of Salvador. We flew there from Rio and took a taxi from the airport into the city on a modern eight-lane, or possibly ten-lane, or maybe even twelve-lane, expressway. You couldn't tell how many lanes there were because the road had apparently just been resurfaced and no lane markings had been painted on it yet. It was just this vast, wide-open, unmarked road, with Brazilian motorists weaving happily all over it at 70 miles an hour.

The game day weather was beautiful, and a big crowd was gathering by a scenic lake next to the stadium. Sophie was wearing red, white and blue clothing and face paint; I was wearing a USA team shirt. There were a lot of Belgian fans on hand, and I made a sincere effort to hate them, but they were annoyingly non-annoying.

It turns out that—speaking of Hellgium—the Belgium team is nicknamed the Red Devils; some of the fans were wearing devil outfits. One middle-aged Belgian guy had painted his face bright red and was wearing an all-red outfit, accessorized with a red cape and giant devil's pitchfork.

People were lining up to get their pictures taken with him. Despite my long-standing hatred for Belgium, I was one of those people.

"OK," he said. "But this is the last one. I need to start drinking."

(It turns out that the Belgians speak English better than we do, which is another reason to dislike them.)

We sat in a heavily pro-USA section, right in front of a large group of flag-bedecked twenty-something American fans who spent the entire game jumping up and down and bellowing songs and chants, as they have seen fans of other nations do. I admired their spirit, but at times it seemed kind of forced and wannabe-ish, like when one of those bands made up of wealthy white middle-aged orthodontists performs a blues song.

Also some of the American fans' songs were, frankly, lame. They kept singing one to the tune of the 1963 hit by Little Peggy March, "I Will Follow Him." Unlike the twenty-somethings, I am old enough to remember when that song was a big hit. I hated it then, and I still hate it, because—this is an objectively provable scientific fact—it sucks. It sucks even more with the strikingly unimaginative lyrics that the soccer fans have given it, which are:

We love you! We love you! We love you!

And where you go we'll follow! We'll follow!

   We'll follow!

'Cause we support the U.S.! The U.S.! The U.S.!

And that's the way we like it! We like it!

   We like it!

Seriously, USA soccer fans? "And that's the way we like it"?

The thing is, there are many popular 1963 recordings that would make much better soccer songs than "I Will Follow Him." Take, for example, the Angels' 1963 classic hit "My Boyfriend's Back." I came up with these alternative lyrics in mere seconds:

America's back and we're better and bolder

Hey la, hey la, America's back!

So you better not try to bite us on the shoulder

Hey la, hey la, America's back!

Granted, that's a tad Uruguay-specific. But it's still better than "And that's the way we like it!"

I don't mean to be too harsh on the American fans. They

made a genuine effort to be original in their chants against Belgium, which included this one:

> *Your waffles are good!*
> *Your team is shit.*

Unfortunately, this was not accurate. The Belgian team was very good—better, overall, than the USA team. But the Americans had Tim Howard, who proved that day that he was the best goalie in the 2014 World Cup, and maybe the world, as well as clearly not a biological human being. He made a record 16 saves, some of them ridiculous. If Tim Howard had been aboard the *Titanic*, the Atlantic Ocean would never have gotten in.

So after 90 tense minutes it was 0–0, which meant the teams had to play 30 minutes of extra time. The Belgians finally managed to beat Tim Howard, scoring a quick goal, then another one. Two goals is a big lead in soccer, and the spirits of the American fans were sagging. But then, with 13 minutes left, the USA scored, making it 2–1, and the American fan sections exploded.

The last 13 minutes were nonstop, sphincter-clenching action, as exciting as any game I've ever seen—the U.S. team taking chances, trying desperately to get the second goal they needed to at least have a chance of keeping their World Cup hopes alive, the players knowing that if they failed, they wouldn't be back for four more years, if ever. In the stands, we were all on our feet, basically just roaring incoherently, getting even louder when it looked like our team might score. And a couple of times the U.S. came *sooo* close . . .

But in the end, they just couldn't get that second goal. (Nobody ever scores in soccer. It's so boring!) The USA's World Cup run was over. In the stands, we applauded the exhausted players, especially Tim Howard. They applauded us back, as soccer players do. More than a few fans were crying. Next to me, Sophie had tears trickling down her face paint. And I have to say, I was moved to the point where I almost joined in the final singing of the Little Peggy March song, although I managed to restrain myself.

As we left the stadium, we passed a Belgian fan, who, seeing my USA shirt, shook my hand and said, quite sincerely, "You did a good job. Don't feel too bad. See you in Russia."*

Damn Belgians.

The next morning (I am skipping over some beers) we took a taxi back to the airport on the Mystery Invisible Lanes Expressway. Our driver was a lovely gentleman in

---

*Russia will host the 2018 World Cup.

his seventies who, having determined that we were visitors to his country, delivered a lengthy informative talk about Brazil, entirely in Portuguese. Michelle was able to understand some of it and translate the gist to me. Among the Brazil facts our driver told us were these:

- Brazil produces many things.
- Fruits, for example.
- Also, nuts.
- Brazil has very good soil.
- There are a great many Brazilians living in Brazil.
- An American who is well known to Brazilians is John F. Kennedy.
- Other people well known to Brazilians are the Pope, Princess Diana and Elvis.

Our driver kept this up for 30 minutes solid, providing us with information about Brazil all the way to the airport. There he presented us with his card, which said that he worked for the John Lennon Taxi Company. He explained at length why a taxi company in northern Brazil was named after a Beatle, but Michelle didn't really follow his explanation, other than that it also involved Frank Sinatra.

From Salvador we flew back to Rio, and from there, after a few more days, back to Miami.

The next World Cup, as the Belgian fan noted, will be in Russia, and I hope to be there, although I'm having a hard time imagining how the Russians could be as friendly and fun as the Brazilians. They lost, but they won. I'd go back to Brazil in a heartbeat. There is *nothing* about that country I didn't like.

Except the damn Belgians.

CABLE NEWS IS ON IT

REMOTE CONTROL: *CLICK.*

ANCHOR: If you're just joining us, something has reportedly happened. At the moment we don't have specific details, but we're following the story closely, and as soon as we have any additional information we will pass it along to you. Right now we're going to go to our Washington correspondent, Rex Farmtrout. Rex, what can you tell us at this point?

WASHINGTON CORRESPONDENT: Bob, I'm standing here in front of the White House, which you can see behind me. At this point I can tell you that we don't have any specific information about what has happened, other than, as you say, something reportedly has.

ANCHOR: Do we know whether the president is aware of the situation?

WASHINGTON CORRESPONDENT: We have received no specific details regarding whether the president has, or has not, been apprised of the situation. I do, however, think we can assume that it is a distinct possibility.

ANCHOR: What is?

WASHINGTON CORRESPONDENT: At this point, Bob, it's too soon to say.

ANCHOR: How would you describe the mood there in Washington?

WASHINGTON CORRESPONDENT: I would describe it as uncertain, Bob. Although at this point it's probably premature to speculate. Again, the White House is right behind me.

ANCHOR: Thank you, Rex, and keep us posted. Joining me now is H. Carlton Prongdale, a former high-ranking government official who we keep here in the studio at all times in a suit and tie in case we need him to provide insights on something. Carl, thank you for joining us.

FORMER HIGH-RANKING OFFICIAL: My pleasure, Bob.

ANCHOR: As a former high-ranking official, what is your take on this situation?

FORMER HIGH-RANKING OFFICIAL: Bob, given what we know at this point, I think it is highly likely, based on my years of experience as a former high-ranking official, that we are dealing with a situation that at this point has too many variables—unknowns, so to speak—to make any definitive assertions regarding possible scenarios or outcomes, if you will.

ANCHOR: If I will what?

FORMER HIGH-RANKING OFFICIAL: I have no idea.

ANCHOR: Fascinating. Thank you, H. Carlton Prongdale.

FORMER HIGH-RANKING OFFICIAL: Please don't put me back in that room.

ANCHOR: We'll be right back with our continuing coverage of this breaking story after this commercial message aimed at the easily alarmed near-death demographic watching twenty-four-hour cable news.

SPOKESPERSON: Hi, William Devane here for Buy Gold or Die. You may know me as a fading, semi-obscure actor reduced to doing commercials, but I'm also a senior citizen like you who is alarmed by all these stories on cable TV news. That's why I invest in gold, and you should, too, unless you want to wind up homeless eating dog food in an alley. Because the world economy is about to collapse and your money will be worthless. That's why we want you to send it to us in exchange for gold. Call the number on your screen right now. I'm not talking about the good dog food, either. I'm talking generic. Take it from me, William Devane. I played that guy in that movie.

ANCHOR: If you're just joining us, we're covering a breaking story concerning something that has reportedly happened. I am joined now by a female co-anchor who is here in the same studio with me but standing roughly thirty feet away for no apparent reason. Janet, what have you got for us?

CO-ANCHOR: Bob, on this high-definition screen next to me is a computer-generated graphic representing the Earth. As you can see, it's a sphere divided into two hemispheres, the northern and the southern, with the northern on top.

ANCHOR: Fascinating. Do we know which, if any, of these hemispheres could be involved in the current situation?

CO-ANCHOR: At this point, Bob, our best guess is that it could be either one, although it's probably too soon to speculate. We do know that the Earth rotates on its axis once a day, so the degree of darkness, or lightness, is dependent upon—

ANCHOR: Hold that thought for a moment, Janet. I'm getting word in my earpiece that we're going back to Rex Farmtrout in Washington for an update. Rex?

WASHINGTON CORRESPONDENT: Bob, I'm still here in front of the White House. That's it there, right behind me. Back to you, Bob.

ANCHOR: Thank you, Rex.

WASHINGTON CORRESPONDENT: No, Bob. Thank *you.*

ANCHOR: And now for this commercial message.

SPOKESPERSON: Hi, Dick Clark here. When it comes to today's active senior lifestyle, there's only one name to trust in home delivery medical supplies: Catheter Planet. They offer great service and instructions written in a really big font. And for you seniors concerned about the looming world economic collapse, they even have investment-grade catheters made of solid gold! Take it from me, Dick Clark: I died in 2012.

ANCHOR: If you're just joining us, we're following a breaking story concerning some kind of development that has reportedly occurred. To help you better understand this story, we've created a dramatic computer graphic logo that we'll put on-screen before and after commercial breaks. Also we'll be playing four somber musical notes as "bumper" music to indicate how serious the situation potentially is.

BUMPER MUSIC: *Dum dum dum dum.*

ANCHOR: And now to get an international perspective on this developing situation, we're going via satellite to foreign correspondent Knowles Cardigan, who is currently in a foreign country located abroad. Knowles, how would you describe the international reaction to this breaking story?

FOREIGN CORRESPONDENT: Bob, I would describe it as subdued.

ANCHOR: So the international community is concerned?

FOREIGN CORRESPONDENT: No, Bob, the international community is asleep. It's the middle of the night over here. I myself am wearing pajamas under this suit.

ANCHOR: Can you speculate on how the international community is likely to react when it wakes up?

FOREIGN CORRESPONDENT: It will probably go to the bathroom, Bob. But it's too soon to speculate.

ANCHOR: Thank you, Knowles Cardigan. Joining me now in the studio is Veronica Bargewater, one of our staff experts that we bring in on these breaking stories to provide specialized expertise. Welcome, Veronica.

EXPERT: Good to be here, Bob.

ANCHOR: I understand you have some video to show us?

EXPERT: I do, Bob. Take a look at this.

ANCHOR: My God.

EXPERT: As you can see, the neonate, which at this point is only thirty-three days old and completely blind, emerges from the mother's uterus and uses its forelegs to climb up the mother's abdomen to her pouch, where it latches onto one of the four teats and begins to feed.

ANCHOR: Is that a baby kangaroo?

EXPERT: It is, Bob.

ANCHOR: So this story that we're covering involves kangaroos?

EXPERT: Not necessarily, Bob. I was the only staff expert available on short notice, and my specific area of expertise is native Australian wildlife. But at this point we can't rule anything out.

ANCHOR: Let's check back in with Rex Farm-trout in Washington. Rex, your thoughts on this latest development?

WASHINGTON CORRESPONDENT: Bob, I'm curious as to how big that baby kangaroo is.

EXPERT: It's 1.5 centimeters, or about the size of a jelly bean.

ANCHOR: Fascinating.

WASHINGTON CORRESPONDENT: If you need me, I'll be right here. In front of the White House.

ANCHOR: Thank you, Rex Farmtrout. And now for this commercial message.

BUMPER MUSIC: *Dum dum dum dum.*

SPOKESPERSON: Hi. William Devane again. If you bought gold in response to my earlier commercial, you have made a huge mistake. Because of very recent world developments, what you need to buy now is silver. You need to buy it right away, before everything changes again. So hurry up and call the number on the screen or . . . Wait! It's changing again! Now you need to buy platinum. Hurry! There's not even time to call! Just throw money out your window and we'll re-trieve it. I'm William Devane.

BUMPER MUSIC: *Dum dum dum dum.*

ANCHOR: We realize we've been throwing a lot of information at you viewers as this story develops. So now to try to make some sense of it all, let's turn to two professional po-litical commentators, representing the left and right wings, to give you a balanced per-spective.

LEFT-WING COMMENTATOR: Bob, at this point the last thing we want to do is politicize what could be a tragic situation, which is clearly the result of the racist, homophobic, anti-woman policies of the Republicans, unless it turns out to be something good.

RIGHT-WING COMMENTATOR: Oh yeah? What about Benghazi?

LEFT-WING COMMENTATOR: You're an idiot.

RIGHT-WING COMMENTATOR: No, you're an idiot.

ANCHOR: Thank you both for that perspective.

LEFT-WING COMMENTATOR: We're also avail-able for paid corporate events.

RIGHT-WING COMMENTATOR: Sometimes, for fun, we exchange roles.

ANCHOR: We'll be right back after this commercial message.

BUMPER MUSIC: *Dum dum dum dum.*

SPOKESPERSON: Hi, Wilford Brimley here. I want to talk to you about something that's very important for all of us senior citizens. But I am God damned if I can remember what it is. I'm Wilford Brimley.

BUMPER MUSIC: *Dum dum dum dum.*

ANCHOR: Joining me now in the studio, as we continue to look for answers in this developing story, is a Magic Eight Ball. Based on what we have learned so far, what do you make of this situation?

MAGIC EIGHT BALL: Reply hazy, try again.

ANCHOR: Fascinating.

MAGIC EIGHT BALL: Ask again later.

ANCHOR: I'm now hearing in my earpiece that there has just been a new development in Washington, so we're going back now to correspondent Rex Farmtrout at the White House. Rex?

WASHINGTON CORRESPONDENT: Bob, we received a report that just a few minutes ago somebody may have seen something fly past the White House, which you can see behind me here.

ANCHOR: Do we know what it was?

WASHINGTON CORRESPONDENT: I don't want to speculate, Bob, but apparently it looked like some kind of small flying animal, like a bird. Or a bat. Or possibly even a large insect.

ANCHOR: Could it have been a kangaroo? As we've established, they can be quite small.

WASHINGTON CORRESPONDENT: At this point, Bob, I don't think we can rule out the possibility of a small kangaroo.

ANCHOR: Is it possible that this kangaroo—assuming it was one—could be linked to this ongoing situation that we're covering?

MAGIC EIGHT BALL: Too soon to speculate.

WASHINGTON CORRESPONDENT: I would have to concur, Bob.

ANCHOR: Good work, Rex. Keep us posted on this developing angle. Joining me now in the

studio is professional pollster Lance Pemmi-
can. Lance, what can you tell us about the
public reaction to this story?

POLLSTER: Bob, our latest scientific poll shows
that Americans are deeply divided about this
story, with 31 percent saying they are moder-
ately alarmed, 24 percent saying they are
very alarmed, 12 percent saying they are un-
decided, and 33 percent agreeing with the
statement that the world is controlled by
a giant invisible telepathic clam named
Ronaldo.

ANCHOR: Can you tell us about the scientific
methodology you use to conduct your polls?

POLLSTER: Bob, we call people at random, and
if they are stupid enough not to hang up
on us immediately, we ask them questions
about subjects they know absolutely nothing
about. We then convert their answers into
scientific-sounding percentages, which in turn
are reported as if they were actual news.

MAGIC EIGHT BALL: Fascinating.

POLLSTER: Sometimes they ask us to sell them
gold.

ANCHOR: Lance, I've got to let you go because I'm hearing in my earpiece that we have a major new development breaking on Wall Street. We're going now to financial correspondent Drake Halyard at the New York Stock Exchange. Drake, what's happening?

FINANCIAL CORRESPONDENT: Bob, we're seeing a sudden, massive, across-the-board plunge in stock prices caused by investor panic in response to reports that there has been some kind of attack on the United States.

ANCHOR: My God. What kind of attack?

FINANCIAL CORRESPONDENT: The reports are sketchy, Bob, but from what I've been hearing from panicked investors, it may have involved an airborne marsupial.

ANCHOR: A what?

FINANCIAL CORRESPONDENT: I assume it's a military term, Bob. I don't want to speculate, but it could possibly refer to some kind of drone, or missile.

ANCHOR: My God.

FINANCIAL CORRESPONDENT: I know, right?

ANCHOR: Do you think this attack could be related to this breaking story we have been following?

FINANCIAL CORRESPONDENT: Bob, it's too soon to speculate, but, yes.

MAGIC EIGHT BALL: Fascinating.

ANCHOR: We're going now to Rex Farmtrout, standing by in front of the White House. Rex, it is now our understanding that the United States has been attacked by missiles.

WASHINGTON CORRESPONDENT: Oh my God. Are you talking about nuclear missiles?

ANCHOR: At this point, Rex, based on what we know, I don't see how we can rule that possibility out.

WASHINGTON CORRESPONDENT: Oh my God.

ANCHOR: Yes. Can you tell us what the situation is there in Washington?

WASHINGTON CORRESPONDENT: It's very tense, Bob. I need to find a bathroom.

ANCHOR: Keep us posted, Rex. If you're just joining us, the United States has reportedly been attacked by nuclear missiles. We certainly don't want to speculate, but the death toll could be in the millions, if not higher. Joining me now in the studio to provide some perspective on all this is Hodge Broner, who hosts the reality TV survival series *Naked and Completely Nude*. Hodge, based on your experience as a host, how horrible is this post-apocalyptic nightmare going to be for the American public?

REALITY TV HOST: Bob, it's too soon to speculate, but if Americans aren't fully prepared to shoot and eat their neighbors, they have as much chance of survival as a moth in a bug zapper.

ANCHOR: Thank you, Hodge Broner. To recap what we know at this hour: Billions of Americans are feared dead following a reported nuclear missile attack. Joining us next will be the cast of *Duck Dynasty*, who will talk about how to shoot your neighbors, and celebrity chef Gordon Ramsay, with some thoughts on how to prepare them. But first, this message.

BUMPER MUSIC: *Dum dum dum dum.*

SPOKESPERSON: Wilford Brimley here again, with an important question for you seniors. Have you seen my teeth?

REMOTE CONTROL: *CLICK.*

EVERYTHING I KNOW ABOUT HOME OWNERSHIP I LEARNED FROM JOHNNY CARSON

✳ ✳ ✳

* * *

Basically there are two kinds of houses:

- **New houses**, which are crap, because they don't build them the way they used to anymore.
- **Old houses**, which *used* to be good, because they were built back when they built them the way they used to, but which today, as a result of being old, are crap.

So whichever kind of house you own, it's going to be some variety of crap, which means sooner or later everything in it will break. Dealing with broken things is the essence of home ownership, and it's exhausting. This is why all civilizations eventually end up in ruins. At some point the ancient Romans got sick and tired of keeping Rome fixed up, so they became lax, and then the Vandals come in and started vandalizing, and then the Goths showed up wearing heavy eye makeup and listening to The Cure, and that was the end of the Roman Empire.

Decay, leading to ruination, is the inevitable fate of every human structure, including your house. Your job, as a homeowner, is to stall the process as long as you can, knowing you will ultimately fail. I am here to help you.

I'm very familiar with house decay. I own an old house, defined as "a house that is nearly as old as I am." It was built back when electricity had just been invented by the Wright Brothers, so the original wiring was primitive. Over the years additional sets of wires were installed by various owners to accommodate the newer, faster kinds of electricity, as well as later technological advances such as the telephone, intercom, cable TV, Internet, Wii, doorbell, etc. As a result, our house is now infested by a vast swarming mass of wires, thousands of miles of them, all of them currently obsolete. I would not be surprised to discover that we have telegraph wires leading to the attic, where the skeleton of a long-deceased Western Union operator is hunched over a telegraph key, waiting for word on the *Titanic*. (I don't know, because I'm afraid to go into the attic.)

Our plumbing is also old, and—as is the case in many older homes—possessed by demons. They live in the toilets. Sometimes I hear them moaning at night, when the house is quiet except for the sound of rats in the attic, gnawing on the bones of the Western Union operator.

Every week or so—more often during hurricane season*— something in our house breaks—lights go out, the phone stops working, an appliance malfunctions, a toilet starts shrieking ancient Aramaic curses, etc. My wife reports these problems to me, because we are a modern enlightened couple who have divided up our household responsibilities equally along non-gender-stereotypical lines:

- **My wife's responsibilities:** Cleanliness, food, décor, clothing, medical care, houseguests, parties, holidays, relatives and all other activities involving human interaction, such as talking.
- **My responsibilities:** Things that break, lizards.

---

*South Florida's hurricane season runs from June through the following June.

We have millions of lizards in South Florida, which is basically a giant tropical Reptile Sex Party. The little buggers are everywhere, including inside our house, where they stand around in a cocksure manner, sometimes upside down on the ceiling, making suggestive lizard motions designed to attract mates. I have repeatedly assured my wife that the lizards are harmless and not interested in us, because they know they cannot have sex with us unless everyone involved is really hammered. But she hates them anyway. She's afraid they will run across her face while she's sleeping. Seriously, she fears this; she has told me so more than once. Here is a verbatim exchange we had, which I am not making up:

> **ME:** Why would a lizard run across your
> face?
> **MY WIFE** (*not trying to make a joke*): To get to
> the other side.

So anyway, when my wife sees a lizard inside our house, she exits the room while demanding that I get rid of the lizard immediately. Which I do, using a simple yet effective seven-step procedure.

HOW TO GET RID OF A HOUSEHOLD LIZARD

1. Get a Tupperware container. I have achieved excellent results with Tupperware's Wonderlier® model storage bowl in the 8¾-cup size, but you should use whatever is most comfortable for you.

2. Holding the container with the open side down, slowly approach the lizard in a non-threatening manner.

3. "I certainly am not any kind of threat!" is something you might remark aloud at this point.

4. When you are within arm's length of the lizard, swiftly bang the Tupperware container down over the spot where the lizard was.

5. I say "was," because by then the lizard—which did not get where it is today by having pathetic reflexes like yours—has already skittered off and is now hiding under a heavy piece of furniture, laughing and exchanging high fives (or, depending on how many digits a lizard has, high fours) with other lizards, followed by sex.

6. Declare something like "Gotcha!" or "Well, I certainly captured THAT lizard!" while holding your hand over the opening of the container

and striding swiftly yet manfully toward the front door.

7. Open the door and make a dramatic flinging motion with the container. Then close the door loudly, but not before anywhere from six to fourteen new lizards have skittered into the house.

Using this procedure, I have successfully pretended to get rid of literally hundreds of household lizards, as well as several household frogs and one household snake. Yes, it's a lot of work, but it's my job. If I don't pretend to do it, nobody will.

The Pretend Method is also effective for dealing with certain other household problems. Let's say that late one night your wife wakes you up and tells you she heard a noise. This is of course your responsibility, because lizards might be involved. Here's what you do: Get out of bed, get a baseball bat (if you don't have one, use a Tupperware container) and stride manfully out of the bedroom. Walk loudly around the house at random for several minutes, then return to the bedroom and tell your wife you didn't see anything. You should tell her this even if you saw a man in the living room wearing a hockey mask and trying to start a chainsaw. There's probably a perfectly innocent explanation. "Don't go looking for trouble" should be your homeowner motto.

Unfortunately, the Pretend Method does not work when something in the house is actually, physically broken. When my wife reports this kind of problem to me, I can't fake fixing it. I have no choice, as a man, but to take meaningful action in the form of picking up the phone and trying to get another, manlier, man, with a truck, to come to our house and fix it.

This is the part of home ownership I hate most. Because here's what happens *every single time*:

The guy with the truck shows up and spends maybe ten minutes poking around. Then he comes looking for me in my office, where I'm sitting in front of a computer, working on a professional writing project. The problem here is that to the untrained eye, professional writing can be easily mistaken for farting around randomly on the Internet.

For example, in writing this essay on home ownership, I needed, for obvious reasons, to find the name of a rock band that was popular with Goths. So I Googled "Goth band names," studied the results for a while and finally decided to go with "The Cure." That was the only band I'd actually heard of, although there were some other good ones, such as "Alien Sex Fiend," "Throbbing Gristle" and "Virgin Prunes."

In the course of this research I found out that there are several sub-genres of Goth music, including one called—I swear—"Gothabilly," which was pioneered by a band called "The Cramps," whose lead singer went by the name "Lux Interior." According to Wikipedia, "Interior was known for a frenetic and provocative stage show that included high heels, near-nudity and sexually suggestive movements. His specialty was the microphone blow job, where he could get the entire head of an SM-58 microphone into his mouth." I did a Google image search and found a photo of Mr. Interior performing this maneuver, and I have to say it's pretty impressive.

The point is, I spent a solid forty-five minutes researching the Goth band question for legitimate professional writer purposes. But if you were to walk up behind me while I was doing this research and look at my computer screen, your reaction would be to think, quote: "He's not working! He's looking at a photo of a man who is wearing only a thong and has inserted an entire microphone into his mouth!"

This is the problem I face every time a guy with a truck comes to fix something. He sees my computer screen and right away I can tell he thinks I'm some kind of pervert who, instead of doing real work requiring a truck, sits around looking at perverted things on the Internet. So we've gotten off on the wrong foot, and it only gets worse, because the reason he has come looking for me, *always*, is to ask me a question about my house that I cannot answer. The conversation goes like this:

> **TRUCK GUY** (*glancing at my screen, which is showing, for legitimate research reasons, a video of a waterskiing pig*): Excuse me.
>
> **ME** (*hastily closing the browser window, thereby revealing an underlying browser window, which, unfortunately, is showing, again for legitimate research reasons, a video of a Japanese game show in which shouting naked men are sliding down a ramp into a vat of mud*): Yes?
>
> **TRUCK GUY:** Can you tell me where your demodulation juncture is?
>
> **ME** (*hastily closing the second browser window, thereby revealing an underlying newspaper website with the headline "Woman Arrested for Engaging in 'Intimate Act' with Lawn Chairs"*): My what?
>
> **TRUCK GUY:** Your demodulation juncture. It's

usually where your main perihelion node
connects with your Boolean overpass valve.

ME (*leaning awkwardly sideways in an unsuccessful attempt to block my computer screen*):
I'm sorry, I don't know where that is.

TRUCK GUY: Huh. (*Pause.*) OK. (*Glances at
screen again.*) Sorry to bother you.

ME: No problem.

When I say "No problem," what I mean is: "HOW THE
HELL SHOULD *I* KNOW WHERE THESE THINGS
ARE? *YOU'RE* THE GUY WITH THE TRUCK! I'M AN
ENGLISH MAJOR, FOR GOD'S SAKE!"

Anyway, what happens next is, the guy goes away for a
while. But I know he's going to come back, and I know exactly why: *He's going to want to show me something*.

"Got a minute?" he'll say. "I want to show you something."

I already know it's going to be something that I do not
care about, and do not understand, and never would be *able*
to understand even if I cared about it, which I do not, because ALL I WANT HIM TO DO IS FIX IT. But Truck Guy
always feels the need to make me look at whatever it is, because he wants to make sure I understand that (a) while I'm
sitting around looking at naked Japanese men, he's out there

dealing with real problems, and (b) fixing these problems will cost me $862.47, or maybe $513.58, or maybe even $1,534.90, depending on what the Random Bill Generator app on his phone comes up with.

So I don't want to go look at whatever Truck Guy wants to show me, but I go anyway, because I don't want him to think I am even less manly than he clearly already thinks I am. I get up and trudge behind him to some obscure part of the house that I have never been to, where he points to some horrendous snarl of wires or dripping pipe or rusted mechanical thing encrusted with lizard poop.

"You see this?" says Truck Guy, pointing to the thing.

"Yes," I say.

"This shouldn't look like this," says Truck Guy.

"Huh," I say.

"Whoever did this, did it wrong," says Truck Guy.

"WELL, I BET WHOEVER DID IT CAME HERE IN A TRUCK AND CHARGED $487.21" is what I want to say, but what I actually say, again, is "Huh."

"I'm gonna have to replace this," says Truck Guy.

"OK," I say.

"And then I'm going to have to install a three-quarters rematriculation grommet to offset the plenary compunction mandible."

"OK," I say.

"And then I'm going to make you wear a Hello Kitty costume and watch while I have my way with your wife," says Truck Guy, not in reality but in my mind, because at this point I am feeling like a less masculine version of Richard Simmons.

At this point you're thinking, "Dave, if you feel so inadequate, why don't you buy some tools, do some reading and learn a few basic do-it-yourself skills?"

Good question! By which I mean: You idiot. Because as a veteran homeowner, I have *plenty* of experience with do-it-yourself projects. When I was younger and stupider, I spent *years* doing things myself. I owned a wide array of power tools, including a very manly one called a "radial arm saw," which was capable of dismembering a water buffalo. I read home handyperson magazines and tackled many ambitious do-it-yourself projects. I built shelves; I installed paneling; I screened in a porch; I even made a desk. At first my projects did not work out so well, but over time, as I gained experience, they continued to come out horribly wrong. People never said: "Is this a new desk?" They said: "What the hell HAPPENED here?"

Because the truth is that no matter what the handyperson magazines say, it takes a certain talent to be a successful do-it-yourselfer, and I do not have that talent. Many people do not. In fact *most* people do not. My authority for that statement is the late Johnny Carson. Back in the 1980s, when I was getting started in my writing career, I wrote a humor book about do-it-yourself home repair, and by a semi-miraculous stroke of luck I wound up promoting it on the *Tonight Show.* I was on for seven minutes at the end of the show, and it went pretty well, because I was being interviewed by Johnny Carson, who could make any guest appear spontaneously funny, including Hitler. When we were done and the band was playing, Carson lit a cigarette, then leaned toward me, and this is what he said, in our only off-air communication: "I used to try to do do-it-yourself projects. (*Pause.*) You can't do shit yourself."

I do not relate this anecdote to let you know that I had a funny personal moment with Johnny Carson and you did not.* I relate this anecdote because Johnny Carson was making an important point, which is that the entire massive do-it-yourself industry is built on a LIE; namely, that you can in fact do it yourself.

The worst offender is Home Depot. This is the giant store chain that runs TV commercials in which eager, attractive

---

*You loser.

young couples, assisted by helpful smiling Home Depot employees, look excitedly at tile samples or pieces of wood and then—approximately eight seconds later, after a brief scene in which they are wielding paintbrushes or drilling a hole while wearing safety glasses—they're standing happily in *a brand-new modern kitchen that they did entirely themselves.*

Really, Home Depot? That has not been my experience with your store. I do not see attractive couples there, eager to tackle major projects. I see beaten-down people whose houses are broken, glumly pushing huge orange carts down endless aisles and standing in utter bafflement in front of vast, daunting displays of house parts they do not understand, wondering whether they should get the five-and-three-eighths one with the ribbed flange, or the seven-and-nine-sixteenths one with the reverse coupling, or maybe the thirty-seven-millimeter one (whatever a "millimeter" is) or maybe just grab the one that says AS SEEN ON TV, knowing in their hearts that whatever one they pick, it probably won't work, and even it does, it will eventually break, because it is part of a house.

You know how drug commercials on TV are required to have disclaimers, so that after they tell you how great the drug is, they tell you it can have negative side effects such as death? I think they should require disclaimers like that on Home Depot commercials. At the end, when they're showing the happy couple in their new do-it-yourself kitchen, an announcer would say: "These people are actors. They are not capable of operating an espresso machine, let alone building this kitchen. This was done by contractors with trucks."

Or maybe just: "Home Depot. You can't do shit yourself."

I'd like to see somebody open a chain of stores called "Reality Hardware." When homeowners wanted to tackle a home-improvement project, they'd go to Reality Hardware and discuss it with a knowledgeable employee, who would talk them through it.

> **HOMEOWNER:** I want to install a ceiling fan.
>
> **EMPLOYEE:** Really?
>
> **HOMEOWNER:** Yes.
>
> **EMPLOYEE:** You want to install a machine with long, sharp blades whirling at high speeds directly over the heads of live human beings?
>
> **HOMEOWNER:** Well, yes.
>
> **EMPLOYEE:** I see. And do you have any particular expertise in this area? Any training in the field of ceiling fan installation?

HOMEOWNER: Um, no, not in ceiling fan installation per se.

EMPLOYEE: In what, then?

HOMEOWNER: I'm a dentist.

EMPLOYEE: I see. And would you be comfortable having a professional ceiling fan installer give you a root canal?

HOMEOWNER: Well, no. But that's a diff—

EMPLOYEE: I'd like you to take a look at this photograph of a recent "do-it-yourself" ceiling fan installation.

HOMEOWNER: My God. Is that—

EMPLOYEE: Yes. His hand. It landed eight feet away.

HOMEOWNER: I think I'll hire a professional.

EMPLOYEE: Yes. With a truck.

HOMEOWNER: Well, can I at least buy the fan here?

EMPLOYEE: We don't sell fans at Reality Hardware. We don't sell any house parts. Or tools.

HOMEOWNER: Well, what do you sell?

EMPLOYEE: Tupperware.

GOOGLE GLASS:
A REVIEW

✳ ✳ ✳

I Have Seen the Future,
but I Had Trouble Reading It

Before you read this review of Google Glass, I want to stress that I am totally "down" with modern technology. I am not some clueless old fart shouting "HELLO! HELLO!" into a mobile phone he is holding upside down.*

I *love* new technology. I am what is known as an "early adopter." Over the decades I have spent tens of thousands of dollars adopting new technology that I used for periods of time ranging from one week to as long as three weeks, at which time it ceased to be as new as it once was, leaving me with no choice but to buy a newer one. I have boxes and boxes filled with old new technology, and still more boxes

---

*OK, I actually have done that. But only a few times.

containing dense, tangled snarls of cables and power adapters that I would need if I wanted to make the technology work again, which of course I never would because it is old.

I have been buying GPS units since the days when they had tiny black-and-white screens that said only: YOU ARE PROBABLY IN EITHER NORTH OR SOUTH AMERICA. I have owned "mobile" phones the size of LeBron James. I early-adopted every single version of the Windows operating system, including "Vista," which summoned hell demons who possessed your computer and played pranks such as changing all your verbs to adjectives, and I *continued* early-adopting Windows versions after that. If Windows came out with a version called "Windows Stab You in the Eyeball with a Fork," I would adopt it.

I currently own seven electric guitars. Seven! Not because I am a good guitar player; I am a bad guitar player. I have seven electric guitars because they are *electric*. I am a huge fan of anything that uses electricity. I have one guitar that, using electricity, tunes itself. You press a button and it makes a noise like *WAAAHOOOOM*, and somehow it is in tune. This is something I have not been able to make a guitar do in over fifty years of turning the little pegs by myself. Tragically, I still have to physically *play* the guitar, so it sounds less like a musical instrument than a device that a sheep rancher would use to repel predators. I hope that someday there will be a newer model of this guitar (which I will buy) that tunes itself and then *plays* itself, so I won't even have to be in the room.

Like many men of the male gender, I believe I have a natural intuitive grasp of how technology works. I am the "tech support" person in my household. Whenever my wife or daughter informs me that some electronic device is not working properly, I utilize my superior knowledge by (a) turning the device off, thereby allowing the bad electricity to drain out of it, then (b) turning the device back on, thereby causing fresh new electricity to flow in and heal it. If this fails to fix the problem, I buy a new one. This always works.

The point is, I consider myself to be pro-technology and knowledgeable about gadgets. So when I heard about Google Glass, I wanted it. I wasn't sure exactly what it did, but I knew it was new, and it apparently involved electricity. It also involved Google, of which I am a huge fan. Google has basically replaced my brain. There was a time when, if somebody asked me a question—say, "Who is Socrates?"—I had to manually think about it. Whereas now I just Google it and, boom, I have the answer. ("An ancient dead person.") Google makes thinking SO much easier. If Google had existed when I was in college, I could have spent the entire four years getting high and listening to Moby Grape, instead of just 87 percent of the time.

So anyway, I got Google Glass. It cost $1,500, which sounds like a lot of money until you realize that it's 100 percent tax-deductible if you write about it in this book.

What is Google Glass? It's a lightweight electronic device—sort of like a high-tech-looking eyeglass frame without lenses—that you wear on your head. On the front right side of the device is a tiny camera and a miniature screen that you can theoretically see with your right eye. There's also a tiny microphone and speaker. It connects wirelessly to the Internet through wifi or a Bluetooth phone. So basically, when you put on Google Glass, you are wearing a tiny "hands-free" computer with direct access to the unimaginably vast information resources of the Internet. Think, for a moment, about what this means.

It means you look like a douchebag.

Seriously, you do. There is no getting around it. My daughter, who has been my daughter for her entire life and therefore has developed a very high tolerance for being embarrassed by me, refused to walk into a restaurant with me until I removed my Google Glass.

If you go to the official Google website for Google Glass, you will see photos of attractive young people wearing Google Glass as they engage in a variety of modern youthful activities—biking, running, golfing, chopping organic vegetables, etc. Google has enough money to buy whatever it wants—Asia, for example—so you know they paid for the absolute best-looking photos of the absolute best-looking Glass-wearing individuals money could buy.

They still look like douchebags.

Am I saying you should not get Google Glass? No I am not. What I am saying is that in weighing your decision, you need to balance the advantages of wearing a vast information resource with numerous "hands-free" capabilities on your head against the fact that you *will* look like a douchebag. Also many people will automatically hate you and/or assume you are sneakily taking pictures of them. Even your friends and loved ones will, at bare minimum, mock you relentlessly. (My own wife, when I put on my Glass, said: "Fifteen hundred *dollars*? Why not just buy joke glasses at Party City?"*)

But let's look at the positives. You can control your Google Glass using voice commands, thereby leaving your hands free for other tasks in your active modern lifestyle, such as chopping organic vegetables. These voice commands begin

---

*For the record, my wife owns an estimated 356 purses.

with "OK, Glass." For example, you might say, "OK, Glass, take a picture." The Glass will then take a picture of whatever you're looking at, most likely a person looking back at you with a facial expression that is expressing the concept "What a douchebag."

You can also use your Glass to (among other things) take video, send and receive emails, check your calendar, get map directions, search Google and view Internet websites—all on a tiny screen! Which unfortunately you can't really see. At least I can't, unless I hold my head very still at a certain angle, looking not unlike the way my dog, Lucy, does when she believes she has caught the scent of a distant turd.

But I am not one to criticize a product merely because it costs a lot of money and makes me look ridiculous and is hard to use. I wanted to know how Google Glass would function under "real life" conditions. So I field-tested it over the course of a weekend in Natchez, Mississippi, where I was attending a wedding. I used Glass to get directions to the pre-wedding brunch, and I am pleased to report that it worked: I was able to successfully navigate my rental car from the hotel to the restaurant by holding my head very still so I could see the tiny map on the tiny screen. Unfortunately, this meant that much of the time I was not watching where the car was physically going. Fortunately—and I mean this as a compliment—

Natchez has a total population of twenty-three, so the streets were empty, and I failed to hit anybody, as far as I know. In Miami I would have killed dozens.

I also used Google Glass during the brunch. One of the other brunchers mentioned that he had heard that the famous bird painter John James Audubon had spent some time in Natchez. This was a perfect opportunity to tap into the vast information resources of the Internet. So I hastened out of the dining room to get my Glass, which I had chosen not to wear into the dining room because the other guests were mocking me for looking like a douchebag. But they changed their tune when I returned wearing my Google Glass and was able, within literally seconds, to inform them that I now needed to "pair" the Glass with my phone. This took several minutes.

Eventually I got to the Internet and was able, holding my head very still and appearing to stare off into space like a psychic communicating with the dead via a bad connection, to read through the Wikipedia entry for Audubon, one tiny screen at a time, until, after maybe forty-five screens, I finally informed the other brunchers that Audubon had in fact spent three months in Natchez in 1823. Unfortunately, by that point the brunchers already knew this and had moved on to other topics, because while I was "pairing" my

Glass one of them had Googled it on his phone, which took him maybe ten seconds. But he had to use his hands. Ha-ha! What a loser.

Perhaps you feel I am being overly harsh. Perhaps you are thinking, "Surely there must be some nerd-tastic place where it's OK to wear Google Glass." You are correct. There is such a place, and that place is: Google headquarters. Outside of that, however, Glass wearers seem to have an image problem. (For details on this, Google the term "Glassholes.")

So my conclusion is that if you work for Google, or for whatever reason do not mind having people mock and/or hate you, and you have a spare $1,500 and would like to have a device that does basically the same things your phone does but not nearly as well—but it's "hands-free"!—then Google Glass is for you. It is not yet ready for normal humans.

I say "yet" because I assume Google is working on a newer version of Glass. In fact Google has asked Glass users to make suggestions for improving it. Here are mine:

- **It should not make you look like a douchebag.** Basically it needs to look more like glasses that a person with at least minimal self-awareness might actually wear.

- **The screen should be much larger and more readable.** You may think this suggestion contradicts the first one, but that's because you're not thinking "outside the box." How about having the screen be a separate piece of equipment, which would be mounted on a service dog trained to trot in front of you? Or the screen could be strapped to the chest of another individual who's usually in your vicinity, such as your spouse or, if you are a busy executive who needs his hands to be free, a member of your staff. Or maybe Glass could have a tiny but powerful projector that would project words and images onto the forehead of whoever you happened to be talking to.
- **It should recognize people and tell you who they are.** This would bail you out of those awkward moments when you encounter somebody you *know* you know, but you can't recall who it is:

PERSON: Hello!

YOU: Hello, um ... (*listening to Glass*) ... your mother. I mean my mother. I mean, Mother! Hello!

- **It should have the capability of squirting fake blood on your forehead.** This would enable you to get out of meetings.
- **It should have X-ray vision.** Come on, Google. You know you can do this. You're *Google*.
- **It should feed you clever insults.** Let's say you're standing in line at Starbucks and somebody butts in front of you. This is the perfect time to hurl a clever insult, but too often your brain can't think of one. At least my brain can't. Usually the only thing my brain comes up with—especially if I have not yet had coffee—is, quote: "Hey!" But suppose Google Glass were programmed so that if you said a trigger word—"Hey!" for example—it would immediately search the Internet for classic insults and clever comebacks and feed them into your ear:

(A person butts in line ahead of you.)

YOU: Hey!

PERSON: Oh, were you ahead of me? Sorry! After you.

YOU (*listening to Glass*): Madam, I may be drunk, but you are ugly, and tomorrow I shall be sober.

PERSON: OK, first, I'm a man. Second, I'm saying go ahead.

YOU (*listening to Glass*)**:** You're so fat, you put mayonnaise on aspirin!

PERSON: OK, then, fuck you.

YOU (*listening to Glass*)**:** I know you are! But what am I?

• **It should be able to shoot pepper spray.** In case the clever insults are not well received.

If the next version of Google Glass incorporates these improvements, plus some kind of invisibility cloak, I will definitely buy it. Of course I will also buy it if it's worse than the current version. I will buy it if it looks like a bedpan attached to my head with a jockstrap. I will buy it if it has an electrical glitch that causes it to burn swastikas into my forehead. I will buy it because it's *new*.

I know what you're thinking: I need help. I need to cure myself of this insane addiction to useless gadgetry. You're absolutely right. I *do* need help. And I am making an honest effort to get it. I have reached out for answers.

But I can't read them on this stupid screen.

TO RUSSIA WITH RIDLEY

✳ ✳ ✳

The Adventures of
Cloak and Dagger

＊　＊　＊

Call me a courageous patriot if you wish, but when my country asks me if I am willing to go on a potentially dangerous mission to a potentially dangerous foreign place where I will run a very real risk of being in potential danger, I do not hesitate. I simply answer, as countless brave, self-sacrificing Americans have answered before me: "Can I fly business class?"

And thus it was that I journeyed to Russia with my fellow author and friend Ridley Pearson as part of the U.S. State Department's American Writers Series program, which is intended to improve our relations with other nations. When I told people I was going to Russia on behalf of the U.S. government, they invariably responded, "They're sending YOU?"

This response made sense, because I have not made my reputation by improving international relations. I have made my reputation by cheap humor stunts such as setting fire to a pair of men's underpants with a Barbie doll. I totally agreed with the people who thought sending me to Russia was a bad idea. But I went anyway, for two reasons:

1. As a taxpayer who has been bitching for decades about how the federal government wastes our money on ridiculous boondoggles, I was excited by the prospect that finally some of this money would be wasted on a ridiculous boondoggle benefiting me personally.
2. I have always been fascinated by Russia.

I grew up during the Cold War. Back in the fifties, when I was in elementary school, I was one of the millions of kids who were taught that in the event of a nuclear attack—which everybody believed might actually happen—we should crouch under our desks. The idea was that our desks would protect us from the atomic blast. (We had sturdier desks back then.)

There was no question who would be shooting nuclear missiles at us, of course: The Russians. They were the enemy.

They were evil. They were Communists who wanted to take over the world and enslave us and make us listen to classical music in minor keys. Russians were the bad guys in the movies, on TV, in James Bond books, in the Olympics, in Rocky-and-Bullwinkle cartoons, everywhere. They talked with thick accents and smoked cheap cigarettes and wore comical fur hats that made them look like frightened wombats were clinging to their heads.

I had reason to dislike the Russians personally, because in 1957, when I was in fifth grade, they beat America into space by launching the first man-made Earth satellite, *Sputnik*.* This event totally freaked out the American grown-up population, because it meant *the Russians were ahead of us.* All of a sudden there was this big push for American schools to teach more science and math, which did not seem fair to me: It wasn't *my* fault the Russians got ahead. Anyway, for years after that, whenever I was in some dreary classroom listening to a teacher drone on about some hideously boring science or math concept that I clearly would never use in real life—the "hypotenuse," for example—I held the Russians responsible.

Then (I am skipping some parts here) in the early nineties

---

*Russian for "little sput."

the Soviet Union collapsed. The winds of freedom blew, and the Russian people were exposed to large quantities of American culture in the form of McDonald's, Burger King, Limp Bizkit, etc. The Cold War was finally over, and we had won!

Or so it seemed.

Apparently, however, many Russians had second thoughts about how things turned out, and now the Cold War has sort of started up again. I will not go into detail on the reasons, because they involve international relations, which for me hold the same fascination as the "hypotenuse." But basically the president of Russia, Vladimir Putin, thinks Russia deserves to be a major world power again, and he sees America as standing in the way.

Putin is not a fun dude. He looks like a Central Casting version of a KGB agent, which is what he once was. In photos, he's almost never smiling: He's usually staring at the camera with the expression of a man who relaxes by strangling small furry animals. He's utterly unlike American presidents, who are always trying to convey sincerity, warmth, responsibility. Putin is trying to convey that he's a badass. He has been photographed engaging in a variety of manly activities such as riding horses bare-chested, catching fish bare-chested, or just generally standing around bare-chested, sending the unspoken but unmistakable message: "My chest is bare."

As I write this I'm looking at a newspaper picture of Putin striding through some tall grass, bare-chested, holding a rifle. I'm trying to imagine what would happen if an American president ever did that. The *New York Times* editorial board, after recovering from its group faint, would demand, at minimum, his impeachment.

But it works for Putin. A lot of Russians like his tough-guy image. They also like the fact that the Russian economy, helped hugely by rising energy prices, has done well in the years he's been in charge. So his approval ratings are high, which gives him a lot of power, which he is not afraid to exercise. At the risk of being informative, I'll quote here from *New Yorker* editor David Remnick, a former Moscow correspondent for the *Washington Post* and a much-respected expert on Russia:

> By 2008, average citizens—far from all Russians, but tens of millions of them—were living better than they had lived at any time in the nation's history. Russian billionaires, like the sheikhs of yesteryear, bought up the prime real

estate of Mayfair, Fifth Avenue, and the Côte d'Azur. And with that new wealth and welcome stability came enormous popularity for Vladimir Putin. His compact with the Russian people, however, was stark: Stay out of politics and thrive. Interfere, presume, overstep, and you will meet a harsh fate.

In 2014, relations between Russia and the U.S., which were already strained, got downright bad. The U.S., claiming that Russian actions in Crimea and Ukraine violated international law, imposed economic sanctions on Russia; Russia, claiming it had done nothing wrong—that in fact the United States was behind the trouble in Ukraine—took retaliatory measures. The Russians were making threats; we were making threats. The possibility of direct military conflict suddenly seemed a lot more real.

It was a tense time, a dangerous time, a time when a misstep on either side could have disastrous consequences. It was no time for fools or amateurs.

This is when the U.S. government sent me and Ridley to Russia.

We knew it was a big responsibility, so we prepared thoroughly for our mission. I don't mean "prepared thoroughly" in the sense of learning facts about Russia or memorizing useful Russian words or phrases. I mean it in the sense of giving ourselves Secret Code Names.

Mine was "Dagger." Ridley's was, of course, "Cloak." We used these names in our email exchanges with our main State Department guy in Washington, Michael Bandler, who became "Scribe"; and our liaison at the U.S. embassy in Moscow, Wendy Kolls, a.k.a. "Lynx." A typical email I'd send them would look like this:

> Scribe, Lynx—
>
> Roger.
>
> Dagger

(Don't be upset if you don't understand this email; that's the whole point of a sophisticated "intel" operation like ours.)

As our travel date approached, Ridley and I wondered if our trip was going to be canceled because of the Ukraine crisis. Maybe we secretly hoped that it *would* be canceled. We'd both heard accounts of Americans in Russia being hassled by the police; we were told that this could happen to us. The State Department sent us each a thick packet of "Alerts & Warnings" for Americans traveling to Russia, which contained this advice:

Travelers should also exercise a high degree of caution and remain alert when patronizing restaurants, casinos, nightclubs, bars, theaters, etc., especially during peak hours of business. Ongoing regional tension associated with events in Ukraine could provoke anti-American actions in an unpredictable location or manner.

Sounds like fun, right? Let's go to a bar during peak hours of business and exercise a high degree of caution! While remaining alert!

I can honestly say, however, that my biggest fear was not that the Russians would hurt me. My biggest fear was that they wouldn't think I was funny. Our schedule had us speaking in a variety of venues—schools, universities, libraries— and about half the talks involved non-English-speaking audiences. This meant we'd be speaking through interpreters. Translating humor into another language can be tricky.

COMEDIAN: Take my wife. Please.

INTERPRETER: You are welcome to take my wife.

Anyway, our trip wasn't canceled. Cloak and Dagger went to Russia. Here's my diary of our visit:

Sunday

We arrive in Moscow on an overnight flight from New York that takes, as all overnight flights do, about four days. At the Moscow airport we slog with the jet-lagged mob to passport control. We can't figure out which line we're supposed to be in because the signs are in the Cyrillic alphabet, which I think might actually be an elaborate Russian prank. It has some regular letters—*A*, for example—but it also has (really) a 3, as well as a backward *N* and various random-looking symbols that look like cattle brands for The Mutant H Ranch. Here's an example of what Russian writing looks like:

Возьмите мою жену. Пожалуйста.

Eventually we make it through passport control and customs. We are met by a driver named Sergei, who speaks no English. *At least not to us.* Ridley quietly observes to me that

Sergei could actually be fluent in English and might just be pretending he's not so he can eavesdrop on us. We have been told that we might be under surveillance while in Russia, and this is definitely on Ridley's mind. He has taken precautions for the trip; his computer has all kinds of anti-hacking software, and he keeps his phone inside a special high-tech bag that takes the phone off the grid so it can't be tracked.

I should note here that Ridley is—and I say this as a close friend—a paranoid lunatic. He's a thriller writer, and he tends to see thriller plots everywhere. He doesn't have a dark corner in his mind; his entire *mind* is a dark corner.

True Anecdote: One time I visited Ridley at his house in Hailey, Idaho, and early on the morning after I arrived we went to a little local market to get breakfast stuff. I need coffee in the morning, so I went straight to the coffee section, where I grabbed a bag of beans and poured them into the grinder. As my beans were being ground into the paper bag, Ridley came over, watched for a few seconds, then said— bear in mind, this was 7 a.m.—"You know, somebody could drop some poison into that grinder, and whoever came along next would pour their beans on top of it, and it would wind up at the bottom of their bag of coffee. They'd take it home, and when they brewed the last pot of coffee, it would kill whoever drank it. Nobody would know who did it."

Then he walked away, leaving me grinding my beans.

That's the way Ridley thinks.

(And for the record, he's a tea drinker.)

But getting back to the diary:

Sergei drives us from the airport to downtown Moscow. If he's secretly eavesdropping, he hears Ridley and me noting that Moscow is a large city. I'm guessing the Russians already know this.

It's also a very clean city—we see no litter anywhere—and it's more attractive than I expected. I had this Cold War movie image of endless massive gray Soviet buildings with gray, sour-faced people trudging past them while being pelted with sleet. But the architecture is varied and sometimes colorful, the day is sunny and warm and the people look like people in any European city. Today they look festive, as Moscow is celebrating City Day, which commemorates the founding of the city 867 years ago. Streets are closed, and happy crowds are milling around, buying food from sidewalk vendors and listening to musicians.

We check into our hotel, the Ritz-Carlton, which is very nice. (Thanks, American taxpayers!) As I unpack my suitcase I watch a Russian TV channel showing Russians doing stand-up comedy. The good news is, apparently Russians enjoy comedy. The bad news is, I can't tell what they think is funny. Some of the jokes involve English punch lines, but they make no sense to me. For example, one comic, after a long buildup in Russian, ends the joke by saying, in English: "Please watch my coat." This gets a BIG laugh. I'm trying to figure out what joke that sentence could possibly be the punch line for. Maybe it has a different connotation for Russians. ("Watch my coat. Please.")

I'm worried.

A bit later, Ridley and I meet in the lobby with Irina Chernushkina, who works for the U.S. State Department. She takes us via the busy Moscow subway to the first event on our Russia tour, an interview on Moscow FM Radio, which is Moscow's only English-language station. It's funded by the Moscow government and caters to expatriates, tourists and students of English. Its format is mostly classic rock music with some talk; its jingle sounds just like an American station's.

We are interviewed by a young woman named Yulia "Juls" Monakhova, who went to Long Island University and speaks excellent English. She's extremely perky. She sounds much more excited about our trip to Russia than we do. After every few questions she plays a song; then it's back to a few more questions, then another song and so on. There are no commercials. It feels a bit surreal in a Potemkin village kind of way—a very upbeat, American-style show on a radio station owned by the government of Moscow. But Juls seems sincere and nice. She asks if we have any requests, and I ask for the Beatles' "Back in the U.S.S.R.," which she plays.

After the interview Irina leads us back to the subway. En route we remark on how lovely the weather is. Irina tells us the government *made* the weather nice. At first we think she's kidding, but she says she's not. She says that on special occasions, like Moscow City Day, when good weather is needed, government planes prevent rain by dropping "cement"—that's the word she uses—into the clouds.

Later on I go on the Internet to check this out and I find that Irina is absolutely correct: Moscow has been dissolving potential rain clouds for years. Here's an excerpt from a 2012 *Pravda* story, announcing that Moscow City Day that year will have good weather:

> The clear sky on the City Day will cost the Moscow authorities 64 million rubles [$20 million]. This is the amount allocated in the budget to dissolve the clouds above the city in case of bad weather. The technology to dissipate clouds

above Moscow was developed decades ago. The clouds will be attacked with dry ice, liquid nitrogen and powdered reagent "cement M-500." The meteorological defense of Moscow for City Day festivities will be conducted from 06:00 a.m. to 24:00 p.m. About 10 aircraft with special equipment will be used, Moscow 24 reports.

This blows me away. In addition to operating an American-style FM radio station, *the Moscow government controls the weather.* I think: Wouldn't it be great if my city, Miami, could control the weather? Maybe it could prevent hurricanes from hitting the city!

Then it occurs to me: If the Miami city government could control hurricanes, it would use them to attack Cuba.

So never mind.

We emerge from the subway near the Bolshoi Theatre, a large neoclassical building with a large statue of Apollo on the roof. Irina tells us this statue has become the subject of controversy. For many years, throughout the Soviet era, Apollo was naked, and his penis was clearly visible, kind of a Moscow landmark. But a few years ago, the theater was renovated, and—in what was seen as a sign of the increasing cultural conservatism of the Putin government—a fig leaf was applied to the Apollo package. This addition was widely mocked, but the fig leaf remains.

As it turns out, the Russian hundred-ruble note features an image of the same Apollo statue, pre-restoration. If you look at this image very closely, you can make out a tiny tally-whacker. A member of the Russian parliament, Roman Khudyakov, recently discovered this and demanded that the note be changed. According to a Reuters story, Khudyakov "said he had been stirred into action when he saw two children looking at the banknote: 'The girl screamed at the boy: "Can you see that? I told you, there is a penis here!" I was shocked, you know.'"

I bring this up in case you think the U.S. Congress has a monopoly on idiots.

Shortly after we pass the Bolshoi, Ridley and I part with Irina, and then a weird thing happens. We're walking along in a crowd and we come across three men standing next to the sidewalk. Two of them are wearing police uniforms and the third is wearing a dark suit. As we approach, all three men turn toward Ridley and me and very deliberately stare at us. Hard. They're not looking at anybody else in the crowd. They're clearly focused on us and they look angry. They're *glaring*.

After we pass them I ask Ridley, "Did you see those guys?"

"Yes," he says.

"What the hell *was* that?" I ask.

"I don't know," he says.

It's an unnerving encounter. We agree that the men clearly intended to intimidate us. But why? Are we being followed? Are we going to be hassled? Maybe even detained?

We're unsure what we should do. But we did not assign ourselves the Secret Code Names Cloak and Dagger for nothing. We assess our situation coolly and calmly, and our course of action becomes clear: We should eat dinner.

We go to a restaurant that has a hand-lettered sign that says "Russian Food—English Menu." I have sausages and beer. Ridley orders something the menu calls "Pigs Knees." I didn't know that pigs had knees, but Ridley says they're pretty good.

He also tells me that as we approached the restaurant, he saw another guy in a suit staring at us.

I order another beer.

After dinner we return to the Ritz-Carlton and go to the rooftop bar, which has a spectacular view of the Red Square area. We order drinks that, if I understand the exchange rate correctly, cost $16,000 apiece. We sip these and watch the moon rise over the Kremlin. It has been an interesting first day.

Monday

At breakfast, Ridley tells me that the second he connected his laptop computer to the hotel network, his security software warned him that his computer was being attacked. He suggests I make sure my security software is working. Unfortunately, I don't have security software. What I have, on my computer, is a sticky film composed of potato chip grease and Cheez-It dust. I'd like to see the Russians penetrate *that*.

After breakfast Ridley and I are met in the lobby by Maria Lvova, who works for the U.S. embassy and is way more educated than we are and also speaks better English. She takes us to our first event, which is at the embassy, a massive stone-and-glass cube in a compound surrounded by high walls, cameras and God knows what else. There are Russian police outside and U.S. Marines inside.

This is actually the second version of this building: The first one, built in the early eighties, used pre-cast concrete pieces helpfully provided by the Soviets. You will be shocked to learn that these pieces turned out to be infested with bugs, and I am not talking about cockroaches. After everybody enjoyed a hearty international laugh, that building was taken apart at massive expense and replaced by this one. They're very picky about letting you take electronics inside.

Ridley and I meet with several dozen embassy people, mostly Americans. We give a talk—this is basically what we'll be doing at most of our Russia events—about how we ended up writing a series of children's books together, the first being a prequel to *Peter Pan* called *Peter and the Starcatchers*. We illustrate our talk with slides, including:

- A picture of me picking my mortified son Rob up at middle school in the Oscar Mayer Wienermobile.
- A picture of Ridley and me playing in our all-author rock band, the Rock Bottom Remainders, with a woman in the audience reacting (as many members of our audience do) by plugging her ears.
- A picture of Ridley and me at a Disney World event in which we are wearing Mickey Mouse ears and grinning like a pair of world-class idiots.
- A picture of Ridley and me at a South Florida bookstore event in which we are wearing pirate hats and trying not to wet our pants in fear while an eleven-

foot-long Burmese python—which the bookstore owner, Mitchell Kaplan, thought it would be fun to surprise us with, so he had the snake handler sneak up on us while we were reading to children and place it on our shoulders—coils around our bodies as we gamely continue reading and pretend to be having fun, which believe me we are not.

In other words, we do not present ourselves as serious literary artists. We present ourselves as a couple of guys who pound out words to pay the mortgage and have some fun along the way. I mention this because in Russia writing is viewed as a Serious Pursuit, and literature, especially classical literature, is revered. Writers like Ridley and me, who crank out books for the capitalist mass market, tend to be regarded as intellectual lightweights. Which we are, of course; I'm not denying that. We are definitely not in the same literary category as, for example, Tolstoy. You will never see a photograph of Tolstoy driving the Wienermobile.

Anyway, the U.S. embassy audience seems to enjoy our talk. Afterward Ridley and I go to lunch with Wendy "Lynx" Kolls, who gives us a detailed briefing on the current state of American–Russian relations, which are—here I am summarizing—crappy. I tell her about the glaring men we saw on the street and ask her if we could be under surveillance. She says it is safe to assume this.

From lunch we go to our next event, a presentation at the Russian State Children's Library, where according to the schedule our audience will be "young readers" and "secondary school students." The library is very nice—big and modern, with lots of fun-looking exhibits and activities for children. We are greeted by museum staff and taken to the bright, airy room where we'll be making our presentation to the children, which will be recorded by two video cameras. Several dozen chairs have been set up for the children, and there's a projector so we can show our slides to the children. We have everything we need!

Except children.

OK, there are some children. Three, to be exact. But they are outnumbered by the adults, which include their parents, Ridley and me, an interpreter, library officials, an audiovisual guy, the camera operators and others. We're hoping for more children, but none arrive. As our starting time approaches and the stench of looming embarrassment begins to fill the room, more adults trickle in and take seats. I suspect they're staff members who were ordered to help fill the room. I picture library officials grabbing random people off the street.

When we finally begin, our Children's Library audience consists of the three children, plus twenty-six adults. Before long one of the children wanders off. So we wind up talking mainly to the adults. They are—as all our Russian audiences will turn out to be—reserved and a bit formal, but also polite, patient and genuinely interested. We're doing consecutive interpretation, in which you make a statement, then wait while the interpreter says it in Russian. (The other kind is simultaneous interpretation, in which you don't stop and the interpreter speaks while you do.)

Consecutive interpretation takes some getting used to, and all the pausing can feel awkward, especially when you're trying to tell a joke.

YOU: Take my wife.

INTERPRETER: Возьмите мою жену.

YOU: Please.

INTERPRETER: Пожалуйста.

But as I say, the Russian audiences are very patient—more so than typical American audiences—and many Russians speak at least a little English. So our talk goes pretty well; we even get some laughs. Also I learn, from one of the children, that the Russian name for Tinker Bell is *Din'-Din'*. This brings my Russian vocabulary to four words: *da* (yes), *nyet* (no), *spasibo* (thank you) and *Din'-Din'*. It turns out that these four words are all you need to get by in Russia, provided that you are accompanied by a professional interpreter.

The Children's Library audience members ask a lot of questions, including some about our careers as writers, which they seem to find interesting. I notice one grandmotherly English-speaking woman who listens intently when Ridley describes how as a struggling writer he had to support himself by working at a variety of jobs, including bartending, fixing cars and cleaning houses. Hearing this, the woman shakes her head disapprovingly and mutters, "America." She is clearly not a fan of capitalism. At the end of our talk, she approaches Ridley and says, "I admire you American writers who work so hard. But I absolutely hate your American president."

This is the only nakedly anti–American-government statement we will hear on our entire trip; as a rule, the Russians—who are fed a steady diet of America bashing on Putin-controlled TV—avoid talking politics with us. Ridley and I both think it's kind of sweet that the grandmotherly woman thinks we American writers work hard, forced by our capitalist masters to tap on our keyboards as sweat pours down our sinewy yet muscular writer bodies.

We have one more event today, which according to our schedule is: "Talk and Q & A at the Oval Hall of the State Library of Foreign Literature (major public event)." The schedule says our audience will be "library patrons, publishers, authors, readers, students."

The Oval Hall is a grand room whose walls are lined with floor-to-ceiling bookcases crammed with works of literature, none of which, it is safe to say, I have read. Our talk goes well; the audience members are attentive, and they get the jokes. We use simultaneous interpretation, with the non-English-speaking audience members wearing headsets to follow along.

During the Q & A we're asked what works of Russian literature we have read. This question will come up during most of our talks, and it's always a scary moment for me, as it threatens to reveal to the Russians—all of whom seem familiar with *our* classical literature—how pathetically little I know about theirs. Ridley, thank God, has read *Crime and Punishment*, so whenever this question comes up, he talks about that, and then usually we're home free. But sometimes I get pinned down, in which case I say, "I read Dostoevsky in college."

This is technically true. In one of my college classes, we were supposed to read *The Brothers Karamazov*, Dostoevsky's brilliant masterpiece that is a spiritual drama of moral struggles concerning faith, doubt and reason, set against a modernizing Russia. Or so Wikipedia says. The thing is, when I was in college, I played in a rock band and had an active social life, plus the sixties were going on, so I did not always have room in my schedule for the actual *college* part of college. I definitely read a *portion* of *The Brothers Karamazov*, but it's a long book containing a great many words, and I did not get through it. I wondered at the time if Dostoevsky got through it.*

Fortunately, the audiences at our Russia talks are not pushy on this subject, and I am able to skate by with glib superficiality. (This basically describes my entire career.)

After our talk Ridley and I return to our Red Square neighborhood for dinner. Seeking to experience Russian culture at its most authentic, we go to a restaurant near our hotel called "La Cantina," which specializes in Mexican cuisine, which I admit is not technically Russian, but in our defense this restaurant is *located* in Russia.

La Cantina has a very busy décor, with posters, flags,

---

*True fact: In writing this essay, I tried to read the Wikipedia plot synopsis of *The Brothers Karamazov* and I could not get through *that*.

banners, jerseys and various other random items covering the walls and hanging everywhere from the ceiling. It is a décor that says: "We are having some fun in this crazy place!" There is a band playing Latin standards. The musicians are positioned on the entrance stairs, so people entering and leaving the restaurant pass through them; one stagger and you could knock out the trumpet player's teeth.

I order a chimichanga. It comes with French fries. I am not expecting much, but I have to say, in all honesty, that this is the worst chimichanga I have ever eaten. It makes me think of microwaved footwear. The margaritas are decent, however. So if you're in Moscow and looking to enjoy a margarita in a banner-intensive environment while watching musicians on stairs perform "Bésame Mucho" as they dodge patrons entering and leaving, I cannot recommend La Cantina highly enough.

After dinner, to cap off our evening of exploring traditional Russian culture, we go around the corner to an Irish pub, which has beer, which I also cannot recommend highly enough.

It has been a good day; to the best of our knowledge, we have not been glared at once. Ridley and I agree that we are liking Russia.

Tuesday

Our first event today is a talk to undergraduate students at Maxim Gorky Literature Institute, which is named for Maxim Gorky, who, as you are surely aware, is a famous Russian literature person, as far as I know. The Literary Institute is an entire university of students who want to be writers or translators. It is also the birthplace of the writer Alexander Herzen, who, it goes without saying, is also very famous; there's a statue of him on the grounds. In fact there are statues of writers all around Moscow. Ridley and I are impressed by this. We try to recall if there are any statues of writers in the U.S. The only one I can come up with offhand is the statue of Rocky, who, granted, was a boxer, but he was played in the movie by Sylvester Stallone, who wrote the screenplay.

The undergraduates, who look basically like American college students, are great. They listen attentively, laugh at the jokes, ask questions. I'm beginning to really like Russian audiences.

After our talk we have lunch and see some more of Moscow. We pass by Pushkin Square, named for Alexander Pushkin, who is a more famous writer in Russia than Maxim Gorky, Alexander Herzen and Sylvester Stallone *combined*.

Pushkin Square is the site of the first McDonald's built in the Soviet Union, a massive restaurant that on its opening day in 1990 served 30,000 customers, a McDonald's record for an opening day.

At the moment, however, it is closed. It was recently shut down, along with a bunch of other McDonald's restaurants in Russia, by the Rospotrebnadzor, or Federal Service for Surveillance on Consumer Rights Protection and Human Well-Being. (Really.) The closings were obviously ordered in retaliation for the U.S. economic sanctions against Russia, but the Rospotrebnadzor claims it was because of sanitary violations. The *Moscow Times* quotes a Russian lawmaker as saying: "I am pleased that Rospotrebnadzor has taken an interest in this important problem. In the future, we similarly will not allow our citizens to be poisoned."

You will be interested to know the identity of this lawmaker who's so concerned about protecting Russian citizens from being poisoned by McDonald's. It's none other than Roman Khudyakov, the same guy who wants to protect the youth of Russia from exposure to Apollo's penis. He's a vigilant dude, Roman is. Maybe when he has eliminated the Big Mac and penis menaces, he can do something about the chimichangas at La Cantina.

We speak that afternoon to Russian literature students

and faculty of the Russian State University for the Humanities. This is our scariest audience yet: These are all serious students and professors of literature.

Our talk does not begin well. When I show the Wienermobile slide, which has been a proven crowd-pleaser in our other talks, nobody even cracks a smile. The students look at the photo—me driving an enormous hot dog—with an expression of mild puzzlement that says, "I enrolled in the Russian State University for the Humanities for *this*?"

But gradually they warm up, and by the end they're asking a lot of questions. Some of these questions suggest that they take our writing more seriously than we do. One professor asks about the major themes in our writing. Ridley and I give each other a look, because we don't really have major themes in our writing. We generally focus our writing efforts on technical plot issues such as how we can end a certain scene with a flying camel pooping on the evil king's head. But we come up with an answer about themes, and the danger passes.

As the Q & A is winding down I ask the students about stereotypes—how they think Americans stereotype them, and how they stereotype us. They say we think they're all drunk on vodka all the time and play balalaikas while bears wander around. Also somebody says "gangsters."

I agree that the vodka stereotype is widely believed in the U.S. (All the Russians I talked to about this claimed it's exaggerated.) I press the students on how Russians see Americans. After some hesitation a young man says Americans are viewed as being self-centered, sitting home and watching their big-screen TVs and not caring about the rest of the world.

Ha-ha! Those crazy Russians, with their stereotypes.

Our final event today is a reception/discussion at the U.S. embassy with various writers, artists and professors. It's very nice, and there is plenty o' wine. Good night.

Wednesday

We do two presentations for students at the Slavic-Anglo-American School "Marina," where Russian students learn English as a second language. They're totally fluent and get all the jokes. While we're packing up, some boys gather around to talk some more. I ask them what they think Americans think of Russians.

"Drinking vodka," they say. "Bears playing balalaikas."

"And what do you think of Americans?" I say.

"Cowboys eating at McDonald's," they say, laughing.

"That is totally accurate," I say.

After our talk the principal gives Ridley and me a brief tour of the school, during which she opens the doors to several classrooms so we can peek inside. Each time, all the children immediately rise to their feet and face us. The principal tells us this gesture of respect to visitors is common in Russian schools. We assure her that it is also common in American schools. Then we laugh.

Our big event today is a meeting with the new U.S. Ambassador to Russia, John Tefft. He was called out of retirement for this appointment and quickly confirmed by the U.S. Senate, which is something of a miracle; in the current bitterly partisan Washington climate, it would be difficult to get the Senate to confirm that the sun is hot. But Tefft is a respected Foreign Service veteran—he speaks Russian, French, Hebrew, Hungarian, Italian and Lithuanian—and he has served as ambassador to Lithuania, Georgia and Ukraine. The consensus is that we need a shrewd and steady hand like him in Moscow. The Russians don't love him, but they respect him.

We meet him at his official residence, a grand mansion called "Spaso House." He tells us he's still moving in, and we're his first visitors. He shows us around the downstairs part of the residence, which is impressive and huge. I think the NBA could play in the dining room.

During our tour Tefft's wife, Mariella, arrives. She's been out walking their dog, Lui, a veteran diplomat dog who is very outgoing, the kind of dog who sincerely loves all of humanity and wants to prove that love by jumping up on all available humans and if possible licking their faces. Ambassador Tefft repeatedly orders Lui to get down, but Lui disregards him. Lui's attitude is, You may be the highest-ranking American official in Russia, but this human NEEDS TO BE LICKED.

PHOTO OF RIDLEY, TEFFT AND DAVE © 2014 BY WENDY KOLLS

We settle in one of the smaller rooms (by "smaller" I mean "big") for refreshments and a chat, during which Lui continues to make it clear, despite repeated scoldings from the ambassador, that he thinks we are just about the most delicious humans he has ever tasted.

The Teffts look like grandparents from Wisconsin, which in fact they are. But they're also savvy, sophisticated players in the world of high-stakes international diplomacy; they have served in some difficult postings, and they're embarking on their trickiest yet. So it's not surprising that the topic of conversation quickly turns to: The Milwaukee Brewers. Tefft is a big sports fan, still fiercely loyal to his Wisconsin teams.

From sports we move to a variety of other topics, including Ukraine, and the current state of relations between us and Russia, which is—and here I will again summarize—crappy. It's an interesting and pleasant hour. As Ridley and I say good-bye to the Teffts—two Wisconsinites and one dog, living in a vast mansion in Moscow, carrying the flag for our team—we sincerely wish them luck.

After we leave, Ridley and I talk about how down-to-earth and genuinely nice the Teffts are. It occurs to me that maybe all this tension between the U.S. and Russia could be eased by some old-fashioned Wisconsin hospitality. Why not? The Teffts could invite Putin over to Spaso House; they could eat some brats, down a few brewskis, maybe catch a Packers game on satellite TV, everybody just chilling on the sofa, with Lui taking advantage of any openings to show Putin some love. It might work! Or it might get Lui strangled. So never mind.

From Spaso House we head to Moscow's Leningradskaya Station to catch the 7:25 p.m. high-speed *Sapsan* train to St. Petersburg, where we will spend the rest of our time in Russia. The trip takes four hours, and the train gets up to 250 kilometers per hour, which is the equivalent of 387 degrees Fahrenheit. Before the sun sets, we get a chance to admire the Russian scenery, which consists of seventeen billion hillion jillion trees.

I like the idea of riding the train. It feels kind of Cloak-and-Daggerish. *Night Train to St. Petersburg.* The only thing preventing me from imagining that I'm in a James Bond movie, hurtling through the night in an atmosphere of intrigue, danger and romance, is the fact that I have developed a case of global thermonuclear diarrhea. So I will not describe the train trip, other than to offer this sincere and heartfelt:

Statement of apology to any Russian passengers who may have used the train toilet that night after I did: Это был не я.*

We arrive in St. Petersburg shortly before midnight and take a taxi to our hotel. I tell Ridley not to expect me at breakfast and sprint to my room. I experience an action-packed night, during which—not to get graphic—I violently expel everything I have eaten in Russia dating back to the chimichanga.

Q. Are you blaming the chimichanga?

A. That would be stereotyping.

Thursday

Feeling weaker but a little better—also much lighter—I join Ridley and our excellent State Department handler in St. Petersburg, Elena Smirnova, in the hotel's rooftop restaurant for our first event, an interview with a print journalist. Afterward Ridley quietly informs me that his computer was

---

*It wasn't me.

again attacked, and that he noticed small microphones discreetly mounted on one of the columns in the restaurant. We speculate on whether there might be microphones in our hotel rooms. If there are, whoever was listening to me last night is going to need years of psychotherapy.

After the interview we depart from the hotel by car, which gives us a chance to see some of St. Petersburg. It is, as everyone has told us, a beautiful city—sort of a cross between Amsterdam and Paris, with a network of rivers, canals and lovely streets lined by mile after mile of graceful buildings, large and small. It has many shops, bars, coffeehouses and restaurants, and a lively sidewalk scene on this sunny, warm day.

Our next event is a talk at St. Petersburg University of Economics and Finance. We of course know nothing about economics or finance, but fortunately our audience consists of students and professors of literature and translation. The talk is in English, without an interpreter, and it goes well. I know I keep noting that Russian audiences are polite and attentive, but it really is remarkable, especially if you've ever talked to a group of American college students who wouldn't look away from their iPhones if the speaker was on fire.

Before our talk we meet with some school officials to

have tea with cookies and chocolates. This has been true of almost every talk we've given; it's a tradition in Russia to serve tea to visitors, always with something sweet. I am struck by the fact that the Russians love sweets, but almost none of them are fat; whereas we Americans are always on diets, and we're a herd of manatees.

We have an opening in the afternoon schedule, so Ridley and I decide to visit the Hermitage, one of the largest and most famous art museums in the world. It's a collection of priceless works, and it's vast. It is said—we hear this several times in St. Petersburg—that if you were to pause for one minute at each item on exhibit in the Hermitage, it would take you *eight years* to see them all. Even if you didn't see everything, you could easily spend weeks, if not months, appreciating all the timeless masterpieces on display.

Ridley and I do the Hermitage in one hour.

Really. And this hour includes stops in a snack bar *and* a gift shop.

In our defense, our time is limited. But also we are—this should be clear by now—guys. We like to move fast and *get the job done*. When we are not encumbered by our families—especially our wives, who always want to stop and *look* at things—Ridley and I can cover a lot of ground quickly. We once (I am not making this up) toured the Tower of London in thirty-five minutes. Our wives wouldn't get a third of the way through the gift shop in that time.

So we move through the Hermitage at a brisk pace, at times breaking into a trot. We are able to mentally process vast quantities of art in mere seconds, using our Guy Vision, which enables us to rapidly scan a large museum sector and summarize its contents:

- *Portraits of portly unattractive men in comical soldier outfits.* Check!
- *Vases.* Check!
- *Statues of naked people standing around expressing the artistic concept "We're stark naked and we don't care!"* Check!

And so on. I'm not saying we fully experience the entire Hermitage in an hour; to do that, we would probably need at least another forty-five minutes. But we have to get back to the hotel to depart for our last event of the day, a presentation to the public at the Mayakovskaya Library, which as you are surely aware is named for the famous Russian writer Vladimir Library. In addition to the usual polite and attentive Russians, our audience includes a cat—Russians love cats—which repeatedly attacks a small patch of sunlight on the floor. Eventually the sunlight disappears, and the cat stalks off, victorious.

Afterward Ridley heads for dinner and I head for my hotel room, hoping that the Russian medicine Elena of the State Department has procured for me will bring peace to the deeply unstable world trouble spot that is my intestinal tract.

Friday

Give it up for Russian medicine: I'm feeling somewhat better today. This is good, because we start by giving four talks, including one for parents, at the Anglo-American School, which is mainly for English-speaking children of embassy employees and businesspeople. It's hectic, but we enjoy it; it's all in English, and the school is a bright, happy place with (thank God) excellent bathroom facilities.

Next up is one of the most serious, and interesting, events of our trip: A meeting with three members of the St. Petersburg branch of the Union of Russian Writers, which was once the Union of Soviet Writers. We meet in their building (they have a building) gathered around a small table, with them on one side and Ridley, me and Elena (as interpreter) on the other. On the table between us are tea and chocolates.

We begin with a lengthy and at times confusing (for me, anyway) discussion of what the union does. To the best of my understanding, it acts as sort of a middleman, distributing money from the government to publishers so that they will publish books deemed worthy by the union. This is of course very different from the American system, in which publishers decide what gets published based mainly on what they think will sell. There's an undercurrent of disagreement in our discussion. Everything is worded politely, but it's fairly clear that they think our system results in a lot of books getting published that are crap (which, OK, is true); whereas we think their system results in the publication of politically acceptable books that most actual humans don't want to read.

We do agree on some topics:

- These kids today!
- This Internet thing!

A few times we even manage to laugh together. But hovering around our conversation is an awareness of the current hostility between our countries. At one point I mention some positive impressions I've had of Russia. One of the Russians, Vladimir Malyshev, responds that I won't be allowed to write anything good about Russia when I get back to the United

States. I tell him that he's wrong, that I can write whatever I want. He shakes his head, clearly not believing me.

Eventually Ukraine comes up. The Union of Russian Writers officially weighed in on this earlier in the year, issuing a statement strongly supporting Putin's actions in Crimea and Ukraine, blaming the problems there on "Western politicians" who want to bring back fascism, and attacking the economic sanctions against Russia.

Ridley and I have no intention of broaching this subject; we're supposed to be having a discussion about writing. But Ukraine and the sanctions come up anyway when I ask what I intend to be an innocent question concerning St. Petersburg's past. For nearly nine hundred days, from 1941 to 1944, the city—then known as Leningrad—was largely surrounded by the German army in what became known as the Siege of Leningrad. It was horrific, the most devastating and deadly siege in world history: Hundreds of thousands of civilians—more than were killed in Hiroshima and Nagasaki combined—died of cold and starvation. In those desperate days, the residents of the city resorted to eating anything they could—birds, rats, pets, sawdust, anything. Some resorted to cannibalism.

This is what I want to ask about. My question is, Does the siege still resonate in the city? Do people still think about it?

Malyshev, answering in halting English, says the siege is still very much part of the city's consciousness. He says both of his parents lived through the siege, and spoke of it often for the rest of their lives. He says the collective memory of the siege remains strong.

Then, suddenly, he connects the siege with the current economic sanctions. His point is that they won't work, because Russians have survived much worse.

"Nine hundred days," he says, his voice rising. "And now we are speaking about sanctions? *Sanctions?* For *Russians?* NINE HUNDRED DAYS!"

Malyshev then picks up the box of chocolates and holds it toward me, as if offering it.

"We give you these chocolates," he says.

Then he yanks the box away.

"Sanctions!" he says.

And then, one last time: "NINE HUNDRED DAYS!"

So he is not impressed by the sanctions.

Our meeting ends with handshakes; we all agree it has been interesting. But I don't think anybody has convinced anybody of anything.

I will say this: The chocolates were excellent, and I was glad Malyshev only pretended to take them away.

Our final event of the day is at the residence of the U.S.

Consul General, where our host is Courtney Nemroff, the consulate's Deputy Principal Officer. This is the monthly Movie Night, in which the public is invited to watch an American movie, usually a classic like *White Christmas*. Tonight, however, they're going to show *Big Trouble*, a 2002 movie directed by Barry Sonnenfeld that was based on my 1999 novel of the same name. The consulate has asked me to introduce the movie to the audience, which is mostly Russians, and answer questions afterward.

The screening is in a downstairs room, where about fifty chairs have been arranged facing the screen. As everyone is getting cookies and tea (of course there are cookies and tea) I'm thinking about what I will say about the movie, which I haven't seen in a few years. I'm mentally reviewing the plot, which involves a series of weird and wacky events in Miami.

Suddenly I remember something: There are Russian characters in the movie. Two of them.

And they are gangsters.

In my defense, I based these characters on a story in the *Miami Herald* about a bar that the FBI shut down after determining that Russian gangsters were using it as a front to sell black market Soviet-era weapons. At the time this seemed like an interesting plot element, so I put it in my novel.

But now I'm in Russia, brought here by the State Department as part of a program intended to foster international understanding. And I have to get up in front of a group of Russians—who already resent the fact that Americans stereotype them as vodka-guzzling gangsters—and introduce a movie based on a book I wrote in which *the only Russian characters are gangsters*.

So it is with some nervousness that I stand before the audience and begin my introduction. I explain that I took many of the plot elements from actual events. When I get to the part about the Russians being gangsters, I see disapproval on the faces of some audience members, and hear some sardonic laughter. I quickly point out that at least the Russians are *intelligent* criminals, whereas many of the American characters are criminals *and* morons. I'm not sure this mollifies them.

We watch the movie, which has a madcap plot involving two criminal morons who mistakenly get hold of a suitcase nuke. Also another character—also a criminal moron—goes temporarily insane when a large toad squirts him in the face with a hallucinogenic substance. There are also goats, and Sofia Vergara. The dialogue contains many references and expressions that I am not sure all the Russians totally understand. But they watch attentively and applaud at the end.

Their questions are mostly about Miami. Among other

things, they want to know if we really have large hallucino-genic toads. I assure them that we do, that in fact when I first moved to Miami a toad the size of a catcher's mitt took up permanent residence in my dog's dish, much to the chagrin of my dog. A woman in the audience tells me that her impressions of Miami have come from watching *Miami Vice* and *CSI: Miami*, and now this movie. She asks if Miami really is an insanely violent place. I assure her that it absolutely is not, most of the time. She looks doubtful. Clearly I have done a lot of good here for the image of my adopted hometown.

Saturday

This is our last full day in Russia, and we have part of it free, so we wander around a bit, then take one of the many boat tours of St. Petersburg. It's another bright, sunny day, and the city looks spectacular from the water, especially the views of the Hermitage and other grand buildings from the Neva River. The tour takes an hour, and Ridley and I enjoy it, although in our hearts we know that a faster boat could have done it in thirty minutes.

After that we do our last event, a short talk and signing

at a bookstore. The crowd is small, yet at the same time few in number. But they're nice and it's fine and we're happy to be done.

We get back to our hotel and go to a nearby Irish pub, our plan being to have a drink there and then go to an actual restaurant for our last meal in Russia. But the beer is good, and the TV is showing a soccer match between St. Petersburg's major pro club, Zenit, and the big Moscow club, Dinamo. Ridley and I have been big fans of Zenit dating back nearly seven hours, when we wandered into the club's official merchandise store near our hotel and bought Zenit T-shirts for our daughters. So we decide to stick around and watch the game and order dinner and, in my case, have several more beers. Soon we are caught up in the game, as are most of the other pub patrons. When Zenit scores, we all cheer; when the referee calls a foul against a Zenit player who TOTALLY DID NOTHING WRONG, YOU IDIOT, we all yell at the screen.

The fact that Ridley and I are yelling in English and the Russians are yelling in Russian makes no difference. For the moment, we're not Russians or Americans. We're humans—mostly guy humans—and we are united by a universal, fundamental human emotion, namely, caring passionately about something that, when you really think about it, is pretty stupid.

Speaking of something pretty stupid, it's time for my:

CONCLUSION

In which I make some sweeping generalizations for a person who doesn't speak Russian and was in Russia for only a week, a large chunk of which, toward the end, was spent in bathrooms

I liked the Russians. I bet you'd like them, too. I'm not saying you'd necessarily *love* them, but you wouldn't say, "These people are the enemy! I want to renew the Cold War with them!"

Granted, we have our differences. The Russians think we're arrogant, shallow and self-centered, and of course we can be all of those things. I think the Russians are a little paranoid, and too willing, out of old Soviet habit, to submit to brute authority, which is why they wound up electing a president who is (with all due respect) a corrupt, macho asshole.

But I don't think ordinary Russians want to pick a fight with us. I think they just don't like the idea of being pushed around on their own continent by a bunch of arrogant,

sanction-imposing American cowboys. This is the hot button Putin keeps pressing.

So we have our differences. But the Russians aren't *that*
unlike us. They're smart, and they have a good sense of
humor. They want nice cars, clothes, TVs, phones. They like
chocolate. They love their kids. They hate the referee.

I think that if left to ourselves, ordinary Americans and
ordinary Russians would get along fine. In fact we *were* getting along fine until our governments started bumping
chests again. I hope that ends soon, although I don't think it
will. I think it's more likely that there will be more chest
bumping, more sanctions, more retaliations. If that happens, it could become more difficult for us to visit Russia,
and for Russians to visit the States.

That would be a shame, because Russia is a really interesting place. I'd like to go back someday and explore some of
its many mysteries, including one I saw early on Sunday
morning as I was leaving. I took a taxi from my hotel at
4 a.m. (Ridley was on a different flight), and as I rode
through the dark streets I was struck by how many people
were still out—clots of partiers slowly drifting home, couples
necking (a *lot* of those), crowds of hardier nightlife lovers
still in and around the bars.

Not far from the hotel we passed a bar called "Meat

Head," which is across a canal from a spectacularly beautiful church called (really) "The Church of the Savior on Spilled Blood." There were several dozen young people on the sidewalk outside Meat Head, but two of them caught my eye, because they were sitting, casually, on horses. As far as I could tell, these were not police horses; these appeared to be just a couple of civilian horses, hanging out at a bar* in central St. Petersburg at 4 a.m. with a couple of nightlife enthusiasts sitting on them. I would have asked the taxi driver what was going on, but he spoke no English, and my limited Russian vocabulary would have made it difficult to frame the question. ("Yes?" "No?" "Thank you, Tinker Bell!")

So there's a lot I still don't know about Russia, and I really would like to go back. Of course by writing this essay, I've blown my cover, so I can't go back as Dagger. I'll need a new Secret Code Name, and I believe I have come up with a good one. It's a name that incorporates part of the history of Russia, but also my own personal experience there and how I was moved by it. Deeply moved. Deep inside. *Way down* inside. In fact as I write these words, I am *still* being moved by it, almost hourly.

Call me Trotsky.

---

*BARTENDER: Why the long face?

A LETTER
TO MY
GRANDSON

＊　　＊　　＊

Dear Dylan Maxwell Barry,

Hi. I'm your grandfather. I'm the guy who, when you were eight days old, held your legs while you were circumcised in your parents' living room.

I want to stress that this was not my idea. My feeling about infants' foreskins is that they are a natural, normal, organic bodily part and, as such, should be surgically removed by trained medical professionals in a room that I am not personally located in. But because your mom is Jewish—not that I am blaming your mom!—you had a *bris*, which is an ancient traditional Jewish ceremony in which a male baby, on his eighth day of life, is circumcised with friends and relatives looking on, after which everybody who has not passed out eats food from deli platters.

How did this tradition get started? To answer that, we turn to a source of wisdom and knowledge that has guided mankind for thousands of years: The Internet. I quote here from kingjamesbibleonline.org, "The Official King James Bible Online," specifically the book of Genesis, chapter 17, which begins:

> And when Abram was ninety years old and nine, the LORD appeared to Abram, and said unto him, I am the Almighty God . . .

Let me just interject here that, with all due respect to God, when He appears to people in the Old Testament, it generally is not a lighthearted occasion. God rarely appears for a fun reason, such as to spell people's names in the sky with northern lights, or turn an entire mountain into fudge. No, the Old Testament God is all business: He appears to people because He wants them to build an ark, or smite an entire nation, or sacrifice something or somebody, or go on some kind of divine-offering scavenger hunt where they have to collect things like goat hair and badger skins.*

Anyway, when God appears to Abram, at first He appears to be in a fairly mellow mood, for Him. He tells Abram that from now on, Abram's name will be Abraham (God can do this), and they're going to have a covenant under which Abraham is going to be fruitful and become the father of kings, on top of which God will give him the entire land of Canaan.†

Sounds like a pretty sweet deal for Abraham, right? He's going to be a fruitful king producer at age ninety-nine, PLUS he gets Canaan, and he doesn't even have to smite anybody!

But then God reveals the *other* side of the covenant, which is, and here I will quote God directly:

> And ye shall circumcise the flesh of your fore-
> skin; and it shall be a token of the covenant
> betwixt me and you.

That's right: God is telling a ninety-nine-year-old guy that to seal the deal, *he has to circumcise himself.* Not only

---

*Really. Book of Exodus, chapter 25, verse 5.

†The biblical name for the land that is now known as Long Island.

that, but God informs Abraham that all of his male children, and all of his future male descendants, also have to be circumcised. And so, that very day, according to the sacred text of kingjamesbibleonline.org, Abraham circumcised himself and every other male in his household. And then, to quote Genesis, "there were deli platters."

No, I made that last part up. But all the stuff about circumcision really is in Genesis. Which raises a couple of questions:

- Why does God have such a bee in His bonnet about foreskins?
- Couldn't they have had some other token of the covenant?
- Like, couldn't they just shake hands?
- Speaking of shaking hands: How do you think the other household males felt when this ninety-nine-year-old guy came wobbling toward them holding a knife and saying, "Guess what God told me to do!"?
- And how come God—with all due respect—doesn't have to part with His foreskin?
- Wouldn't *The Foreskin of God* be an excellent name for a science-fiction novel?

But these are questions best left to theologians. The point, Dylan, is that circumcision is an important Jewish tradition, which is why, as the son of a Jewish mom, you had a *bris*. And as your grandfather, I was chosen by your parents for the honor of being the *sandek*, who is the person who holds the baby while the actual snipping is done by the *mohel*, which is Hebrew for "snipper." Your specific *mohel*, a nice man named Philip Sherman, told me that he had done 21,000 circumcisions, which—to put that mind-boggling number in perspective—is the equivalent of circumcising every member of the boy band One Direction *4,200 times.*

So you were in experienced hands, although I personally did not watch the procedure. I focused on your face, and I have to say, except for a couple of totally understandable yelps, you took it like a man. Whereas I cried like a baby.

Anyway, you're my first grandchild, so I feel it's my duty to offer you some grandfatherly wisdom in the form of this letter, which I'll ask your parents to keep for you in a safe place until you're older and less likely to get poop on it. My goal, in writing this letter, is to pass along to you the important knowledge I have accumulated in my sixty-seven years on this Earth. Here's the main thing I have learned:

You do not need to refrigerate ketchup or mustard.

Dylan, this is something that I believe deeply, both as a

person and as a human being. It is not, however, a popular opinion. Many people believe that if left unrefrigerated, ketchup and mustard will go bad. But one thing you must learn is that just because "many people" believe something, that does not make them right. Many people believe in astrology. Many people believe that their cats actually like them. Many people believe that the New York Yankees are not the agents of Satan. Many people believe that "light beer" is a form of beer. Many people voluntarily purchase recordings by Barry Manilow.

Am I saying that all of these people are stupid? Of course not. Some of them are insane. But my point, Dylan, is: Don't just follow the crowd. Think for yourself. Someday, when you are older and no longer spurting fluids out of all your orifices at random, you will start going to restaurants. When you do, I want you to notice two things: (1) the ketchup and mustard are kept sitting out all day in a room that is, by definition, room temperature; and (2) the customers are not keeling over and dying from condiment-transmitted diseases. Instead, they are enjoying room temperature ketchup and mustard on their food. Because, as has been shown in countless laboratory studies,* THIS IS PERFECTLY SAFE. Nev-

---

*This might not technically be true, but it adds strength to my argument.

ertheless, in households all over America, millions of people routinely ruin perfectly good hamburgers and hot dogs by putting cold ketchup and mustard on them.

Don't be one of those people, Dylan. Say no to cold ketchup.

Also: Be nice to people; don't be rude. This is almost as important as not refrigerating ketchup and mustard. It seems like an obvious concept, right? *Be nice; don't be rude.* But some people have trouble grasping it. Some people are nice only to people they want to impress, or to people they think can help them. But when they're dealing with somebody they consider to be not useful, or unimportant, especially if that person pretty much has to take the abuse—an underling, a salesclerk, a waiter, a flight attendant—these people feel free to be rude. These people are what we call "jerks."*

Don't be a jerk, Dylan. Be nice to everybody. If somebody turns out to be a jerk, you can stop being nice to that person. But always start with nice. Say "please" and "thank you." Share. Take turns. Don't bully, and don't hit people, unless they are bullying you, in which case go ahead and belt them.

---

*Actually, we call them "assholes," but I don't want you learning that word from your grandfather.

Never butt in line. Yes, sometimes this will get you ahead. But the people you butted in front of will know you're a jerk, and they will stare hatefully at the back of your neck, and the hate rays emitted by their eyeballs will build up inside you and eventually, down the road, cause your goiter to explode.

Or so I choose to believe.

Likewise, do not be one of those people who are constantly standing up and blocking the view of the people behind them at concerts and sporting events. It's OK to stand up when everybody else is standing up; crowds are pretty good at figuring out, as a group, when to do this. But there always seem to be some people—and they always seem to be seated in front of you—who believe they are entitled to stand up any old time they feel like it, which is a lot, because they are REAL FANS, by which I mean drunk. If you ask them to sit down, they will either ignore you, or tell you that if you were a REAL FAN, like them, you would be standing, too.

As a result, the people behind them have no choice but to crush their skulls with a ball-peen hammer.

No, Dylan, that would be wrong, by which I mean technically illegal. The people behind them have no choice but to stand up—thereby blocking the view of the people behind *them*—or spend the concert or sporting event staring at the idiots' butts, which will eventually, down the road, because of all the eyeball hate rays beamed at them, develop hemorrhoids the size of mature cantaloupes, or so I choose to believe.

But the point is, don't be one of those people.

Be loyal to your friends. Popularity is way overrated; friendship is not.

Be considerate. Clean up after yourself. Don't leave your trash for other people to deal with. Don't force other people to listen to your phone conversations or your music. Signal your turns. If you're in the left lane, and people keep passing you on the right, get out of the left lane. If you use the toilet, flush the toilet. How hard is that, right? *Flush the damn toilet.* You'd be amazed how many people don't. I'd call these people "pigs," but I believe that if pigs had toilets, they would have enough class to flush them.

Don't be a know-it-all. There will come a time—probably when you're in college—when you'll start to believe you really *do* know it all, and you will become passionate about your beliefs, and you will be insufferable. But trust me: When you leave college and have to get an actual job, you will discover that there's a whole lot of stuff you don't know, and you will be on your way to becoming an adult.

Remember that being offended is not the same thing as

being right. And even if you're pretty sure you're right about something, be cool about it. If you want to get people to agree with you, *talk* to them, and then—even more important—*listen* to them. Don't lecture them; don't hector them; for God's sake, don't form a demonstration and shout mindless slogans at them. People do not respond well to being lectured. People are turned off by perpetual outrage and smug moral preening. This is one reason why everybody hates Washington, D.C.

A few more things:

- Don't brag.
- Don't whine.
- Floss your teeth. (Once you get teeth, I mean.)
- You do not need the extended warranty.
- VERY IMPORTANT: If you want to impress a woman, do not buy her a gift that has a plug.
- Finally, always remember that there is a fine line between being trendy and being a douche.

So that's it, Dylan. That's my wisdom. To be honest, it might not all be correct. The only thing I'm 100 percent sure of is the part about the ketchup and mustard. But I hope you find this helpful, and I hope you live a long and happy life. I hope you have children as terrific as mine, and I hope they have children, so that one day you might get a chance to write a letter to your first grandchild. Maybe, if it's a boy, and he has a *bris*, you'll even be asked to be the *sandek*. If you are, I have one more piece of wisdom for you:

It's OK to cry.

Much love,
Grandpa Dave